The Diary of a Civil War Bride

Library of Southern Civilization

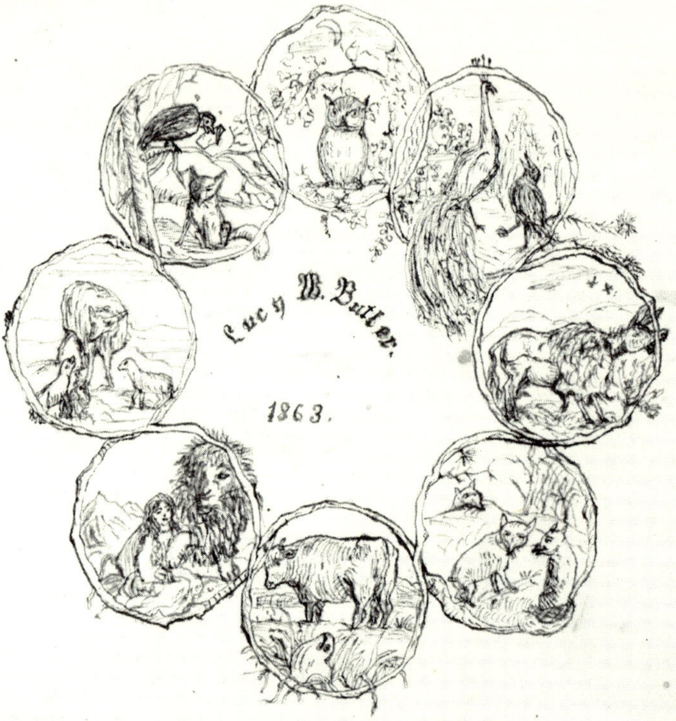
Lucy B. Butler.
1863.

The DIARY of a CIVIL WAR BRIDE

Lucy Wood Butler
of Virginia

Edited by
KRISTEN BRILL

LOUISIANA STATE UNIVERSITY PRESS
BATON ROUGE

Published by Louisiana State University Press

Manufactured in the United States of America
First printing

DESIGNER: *Mandy McDonald Scallan*
TYPEFACE: *Ingeborg*
PRINTER AND BINDER: *Sheridan Books, Inc.*

Frontispiece featuring Lucy Wood Butler's sketches used courtesy of Charles E. B. Glenn.

Library of Congress Cataloging-in-Publication Data
Names: Butler, Lucy Wood, 1841–1921, author. | Brill, Kristen, 1986– editor.
Title: The diary of a Civil War bride : Lucy Wood Butler of Virginia / edited by Kristen Brill.
Description: Baton Rouge : Louisiana State University Press, 2018. | Includes index.
Identifiers: LCCN 2017009680| ISBN 978-0-8071-6741-0 (cloth : alk. paper) | ISBN 978-0-8071-6742-7 (pdf) | ISBN 978-0-8071-6743-4 (epub)
Subjects: LCSH: Butler, Lucy Wood, 1841–1921—Diaries. | Albemarle County (Va.)—Social life and customs—19th century. | United States—History—Civil War, 1861–1865—Social aspects. | United States—History—Civil War, 1861–1865—Women. | Married people—Virginia—Albemarle County—Biography. | Butler, Waddy, –1863.
Classification: LCC F232.A3 B87 2018 | DDC 975.5/482—dc23
LC record available at https://lccn.loc.gov/2017009680

The paper in this book meets the guidelines for permanence and durability of the Committee on Production Guidelines for Book Longevity of the Council on Library Resources. ♾

Contents

Acknowledgments

This project would never have come to fruition without the tireless help and support of the archival staffs at the Virginia Historical Society and the Albert and Shirley Smalls Special Collection Library at the University of Virginia. I am grateful for your endless patience, knowledge, and advice.

Most important, I would like to thank the family of Lucy Wood Butler for their generosity in making these materials available to a wider audience.

Note on the Text

Identical typescript copies of the letters and diary of Lucy Wood Butler are held in the Lomax Family Papers at Virginia Historical Society, the Albert and Shirley Smalls Special Collections Library at the University of Virginia, and the Louis Round Wilson Special Collections Library at the University of North Carolina (UNC)–Chapel Hill. The originals were lent to these libraries by Lucy Wood Butler's family for photocopying in the mid-twentieth century and were returned to the family. The documents remain in their private possession. The original handwritten diary is also in the possession of Butler's family, but this has been missing for several years.

Given that these pages appear in typescript (as opposed to handwritten text), some letters are missing from the correspondence exchange, and a handful of footnotes accompany the diary's text, the diary most likely sustained editorial revision between its last entry in 1863 and the earliest record of its donation to an archive for photocopying (UNC, 1946). Lucy Wood Butler herself could have made these revisions and/or created a typescript copy of the text, or another person with access to her diary, before or after her death in 1921, could have done so. These editorial changes could have been made to ensure the clarity of prose and presentation of ideas to future readers or to underscore or understate specific issues, or the diary itself, as a material object, may have physically deteriorated to a degree that made it difficult to decipher the existing text. In her personal papers at the University of Virginia, there is no record of Butler pursuing commercial publication of the diary.

In terms of my own editorial intervention for publication in the twenty-first century, the following pages present the text of Lucy Wood Butler's Civil War era diary identically as it appears in the archival collections, including her uncorrected spelling, emphasis, and grammar.

In this way Butler's voice is presented with as little editorial intervention (from me) as possible: This is Lucy Wood Butler's first-person narrative, not a third-person narrative of Lucy Wood Butler.

The diary makes frequent references to the numerous people Butler encountered in her everyday life. I provide a footnote with biographical information only when the newly introduced person is relevant to the narrative.

The Diary of a Civil War Bride

INTRODUCTION

ENGAGINGLY INTERWEAVING THE PRIVATE WITH THE public, the personal with the political, Lucy Wood Butler fashioned a revealing and poignant diary of her life in Civil War Virginia. Her first-person narrative illustrates, and at times complicates, the wider Confederate narrative of gender, class, and identity politics in the first two years of the national conflict. In this way the diary not only tells her own *individual* story; it also tells the story of the *collective* Confederate republic.

Lucy Wood was born on November 14, 1841, to John Wood Jr. (1811–99) and Eliza Jane Harper Wood (1817–1907) and raised in Albemarle County, Virginia. She was the third of ten children; two died in childbirth.[1] In the 1840 census, the year before Lucy's birth, the Wood family owned five slaves. In the 1840 and 1850 censuses her father listed his profession as a farmer; by 1860 he would be working in the insurance industry. The Wood family lived in the rural community of Ivy, the birthplace of explorer Meriwether Lewis, five miles west of Charlottesville and Thomas Jefferson's University of Virginia. Jefferson's iconic neoclassical plantation home, Monticello, as well as James Monroe's Ash Lawn–Highland were just outside the town. Charlottesville was situated between the two warring capitals: The Confederate capital, Richmond, was seventy miles to the southeast, and the Union capital, Washington, D.C., was one hundred miles to the northeast. The town surrendered to the Union on March 3, 1865, a little over a month before the Confederacy's surrender at Appomattox on April 7.

In 1860 approximately 3,000 residents lived in Charlottesville (compared to over 30,000 in Richmond). In greater Albemarle County the enslaved population outnumbered the slaveholding population: There were 13,196 enslaved African Americans and 12,103 whites.[2] The Woods were a leading family in the county; they were often engaged in charitable causes and hosted events and local celebrations. The famed Kentucky statesman Henry Clay even wrote to John Wood Jr. in September 1846. Clay recognized Wood as an unofficial representative of Albemarle County, expressing admiration and affection for both Wood as well as the county.[3]

Lucy Wood met Washington "Waddy" Butler (b. 1840) when he was a student at the University of Virginia in the late 1850s. After university Waddy returned to his native Florida to pursue a career as a lawyer, and he continued a prolific correspondence with Lucy in Charlottesville. The advent of war would soon drastically change southern courtship rituals, making relationships for upper- and middle-class white women more short-lived and casual than in the antebellum tradition. Still, Waddy Butler and Lucy Wood maintained a fairly conventional antebellum courtship, then engagement, in the final months before the war.[4] Their exchange of letters from May 1859 to May 1861 shows individual, emotional responses to the national political crisis of secession. The disunion of the United States is framed through the union of Lucy Wood and Waddy Butler. These two parallel narratives show the humanistic dimension of the conflict; this was the story not just of warring regions but of human actors negotiating the terms of their own lives affected by dire political circumstances. In response to his marriage proposal, Wood wrote to Butler in October 1860, "I feel so sure that a great calamity will ere long befall us and our country that I dread the idea of making plans for the future."[5]

With the outbreak of war, Butler was mustered into the Second Florida Regiment as an adjutant.[6] After a courtship of two years, on July 3, 1861, Lucy Wood, at the age of nineteen, married Waddy Butler.[7] Shortly after their austere wedding—"[I] dressed as simply as possible, for I would not have worn anything handsome or expensive at such a time as this"—Waddy Butler departed to his regiment, and Lucy Wood Butler remained at her family home near Charlottesville.[8] There is little record of Lucy Butler's wartime life other than her diary. Nevertheless, as a stand-alone document, her diary reveals a wealth of information: It is a coming-of-age narrative not just of its writer but of the divided nation in which she lived.

Just as Waddy Butler tried to navigate his new life within the structure and hierarchy of the Confederate army, in a parallel vein Lucy Butler tried to navigate her new life on the Confederate home front. She immediately sought to find a meaningful place for herself in the war effort. Like most women of her class, she relentlessly engaged in sewing, preparation of food, nursing, and prayer to contribute to the cause and support the men on the frontlines. In May 1861 she offered a proud and triumphant description of southern women's wartime duties on the home front:

> Our needles are now our weapons, and we have a part to perform as well as the rest: we must make our men comfortable, we must encourage them by brave words and keeping stout hearts, we must try to turn their hearts to guider of all destinies, and we must cry mightily unto Him day and night, and must trust in Him to deliver us. Yes, yes, we women have mighty work to perform for which we will be responsible. We have no glory, no fame to gain on earth, but it is ours to calm the fierce feeling of hatred and revenge, to be with and minister to the dying and the wounded; ours to point and lead the way for others—to attain for ourselves a glorious eternity and victory over our worst enemy.[9]

When Lucy Butler did allow herself time for leisure, reading and writing were her passions. She was an avid reader: Her reading list for the first half of 1863 reads more like a college syllabus, including such works as a collection of essays on Goethe and a history of the Girondists.[10] She was educated and well read: Her diary is laced with references to literature, including works by John Milton and Lord Byron.[11] Her prose is clear and concise. Her narrative is often spliced with eloquent, poetic passages pontificating on the culture of war in a more universal context: "Little by little did the cloud spread, blacken, and advance, and now it has burst upon us . . ."[12] Such passages show strong stylistic talent and literary flair as well as a nuanced understanding of the ways in which the politics of violence and conflict function on a more universal level.

From the home front Lucy Butler provided vivid and detailed observations on military affairs—namely, companies stationed locally and the orders of the Charlottesville companies.[13] Given the underdevelopment of communication and transportation networks in the South, her comments on events outside of her immediate geographic community are often unreliable. She frequently had to correct earlier statements and insert missing information. The narrative itself is an unwitting documentation of one of the Confederacy's major weaknesses: its inability to effectively transport information, as well as people and supplies, across the region.

In May 1863, nearly two years after starting her diary, Waddy Butler was killed at the Battle of Chancellorsville.[14] Lucy Butler received word of his death early that summer. On July 3 she concluded her diary: "Just two years since tonight I was a bride . . . though many had already rushed to arms, we were too happy to take warning. Since that night . . . rivers of blood have been poured forth, and I, I am left alone without hope."[15] Like the Confederacy, she had started the war with optimism and hope, but that fleeting euphoria soon gave way to the realities of conflict and sacrifice. First her marriage, then the Confederacy, would collapse around her.

For the rest of the war there is little record of Lucy Butler beyond her husband's death. One notable exception is a letter sent to her by the celebrated southern writer William Gilmore Simms in January 1865. After a convalescence at their home earlier in the war, Simms expressed his gratitude and affection for the Wood family in a letter addressed to Lucy: "I think of your family's much kindness to me, I cannot but believe, that you all look upon me more, as a friend, than, a mere beneficiary . . . I have been wishing ever since I have been here for something to happen which would carry me to Richmond, so that I may be able to see you all again."[16]

Unsurprisingly, after the war Butler mourned her personal as well as the national loss. In 1866 she implored a friend, George Brown from Centreville, Florida, to inquire about the Second Florida Regiment, the regiment of her late husband.[17] In the decades that followed, however, her comments on the war become increasingly rare. She maintained a correspondence with her extensive family network, mainly on the East Coast, and an active calendar of social engagements. Among her correspondents were Ellen Maury Slayden, wife of Congressman James Luther Slayden, as well as various members of Congressman John W. Fishburne's family.[18] She continued to reside in the Charlottesville area and made a trip to the Philadelphia Exposition in 1876. She also spent time in Baltimore.[19]

Keeping busy, in the late 1870s she considered opening a local school with her sister Lydia. By 1900 Butler hosted paying boarders at the Woods's Spring Hill residence in Ivy.[20] Early in the twentieth century, in the *New York Tribune* and later reprinted in the *Danville Register*, writer Beverly Smith provided a romantic description of Butler's small community in Albemarle County, laced with the mythology of the Old South: "Ivy had everything. It didn't have prosperity, but that was irrelevant . . . it had a curious and happily varied population. About two-thirds of the white population were native Virginians, and if they had been impoverished by the Civil War I never hear the fact mentioned—in itself a record . . . The negro population lived in the utmost amity with the whites. A lynching there would have been unconceivable, unless of a man who himself suggested a lynching."[21]

Lucy Wood Butler lived her entire life in Albemarle County, from birth until death. After the death of Waddy, she never remarried or had children. She died at Spring Hill on May 25, 1921, at the age of seventy-nine.

Lucy Wood Butler's diary is an invaluable contribution to first-person narratives and women's writings of the Civil War. While there has been a greater appreciation for women's history and women's accounts of the war since the turn to the social history of the conflict in the 1960s and the emergence of gender history in the 1980s, this diary offers a fresh and underrepresented perspective on a number of key areas.[22] First, in terms of socioeconomic status the diary provides an account from a woman outside of the elite class: Most southern women's wartime diaries were written by the wives or daughters of planters who owned twenty or more slaves. The multiple editions and prolific publication record of the diary of Mary Boykin Chesnut, for example, is emblematic of the overrepresentation of the experiences of the wealthiest white women in Civil War society.[23] Chesnut's triumphs and travails are not representative of the war experiences for the middling classes, including those of women like

Butler. In her introduction to the wartime diary of Judith White McGuire, Jean Berlin notes the need for less "exceptional" and more "ordinary" accounts of war. Judith White McGuire was the daughter of a Virginia Supreme Court justice, and her husband, John McGuire, was a member of the Virginia Secession Committee (which Butler herself attended). Like Butler, while her family was certainly middle class, they were not members of the elite. Berlin argues: "While Chesnut was an exceptionally perceptive and literate woman, McGuire was more typical of her class and gender, and in that very ordinariness lies the value of her journal. For we need to understand the greater number of McGuires if we are to better understand the important role Southern women played in the Civil War."[24] In this way the diary of Butler, like the diary of McGuire, serves as a corrective counterbalance to the overrepresented portrayals of the most elite women in society.

Second, the diary offers a particularly humanistic portrayal of the national crisis: The divorce of the states is paralleled to the marriage of Waddy Butler and Lucy Wood. The fluency with which the diary oscillates between the personal and the political shows how the high politics of the secession crisis permeated the private sphere on more emotional terms. One way in which the lines between the personal and the political, the private and the public, blurred was the use of family rhetoric to describe and imagine the secession crisis, something that was prevalent across society and on both sides of the sectional divide. Returning to Mary Chesnut, the iconic diarist equated the secession crisis with divorce: "We are divorced because we have hated each other so. If we could only separate, a 'separation à l'agréable,' as the French say it, and not have a horrid fight for divorce."[25] Likewise, Abraham Lincoln employed the language of family and household to illustrate the imminent breakages in the nation. In his first inaugural address, on March 4, 1861, Lincoln called for preserving the Union: "Physically speaking, we [the states] can not separate . . . A husband and wife may be divorced and go out of the presence and beyond the reach of each other, but the different parts of our country can not do this."[26] Three years earlier, in his June 16, 1858, "House Divided" speech, running against Democrat Stephen A. Douglas for the Illinois Senate's junior seat, Lincoln utilized visions of domestic disorder and rupture to issue an ominous forecast for the nation: "A house divided against itself cannot stand. I believe this government cannot endure, permanently, half slave and half free. I do not expect the Union to be dissolved; I do not expect the house to fall; but I do expect it will cease to be divided."[27] The metaphor that Chesnut and Lincoln used for rhetorical effect Butler actually lived every day of the war. Her experience of war was her experience of marriage; her experience of marriage was her experience of war. The struggle to preserve her newly established marriage coincided with the struggle to sustain the newly established Confederacy. Both projects were ultimately doomed: Butler's marriage ended with the death of her husband in May 1863, and the Confederacy ended with its surrender at Appomattox in April 1865.

Thematically, the diary offers key interventions into social and cultural studies of the southern home front, specifically in terms of the changing politics of class, race, and gender identity with the advent of war. Butler recognized her exceptional circumstances of living through the Civil War and felt compelled to record this watershed event. Yet she saw herself as an ordinary individual, not qualified to accurately chronicle the war. Wartime planter women frequently expressed a lack of confidence and assurance in their writing abilities; they alluded to a feeling of discomfort and embarrassment were someone else to read their work. The diarists wove apologetic disclaimers throughout their narratives, lamenting their inadequacy as writers in terms of both historical content and prose style. In March 1863 Butler questioned her ability to effectively communicate her thoughts and experiences of the war: "How like my words are to a poor picture, mere symbols or signs of the inward thought as the picture is composed of the signs of nature that would fain be imitated; though often the language I use consists of mere sounds that none of my audience can interpret and I can scarcely understand myself. Oh, would that I could express my thoughts and my feelings!"[28] Diarists were acutely aware of their shortcomings as historians and writers.[29] As Amy Wink notes, this was not a characteristic unique to Civil War diarists but was symptomatic of the collection of American women's diaries throughout the nineteenth century as a result of women's constraint and disempowerment under a patriarchal social structure.[30]

In terms of young women's education, some southern families initially sent their daughters to female academies in the North. As the antebellum years progressed and more female academies were established in the South, they also had the option to send their daughters to institutions within the region.[31] Southern women could also receive tutoring in their own private homes. The goal of young women's education was twofold. Parents encouraged their daughters to excel academically, like their brothers, gaining a mastery of the classics and foreign languages.[32] But they also desired their daughters to master "feminine accomplishments" such as music, drawing, and letter writing.[33] Southern women's education was designed to mold them into the highest-quality wives for suitors, which required the amalgamation of academic and feminine accomplishments.

Such young women often kept diaries during the antebellum period. They were encouraged by their mothers to maintain the practice in order to foster gentility and education.[34] The diaries of these young, educated women tended to focus on personal issues such as religion, family, and self-improvement; generally, they abstained from broader societal and political commentaries. Elizabeth Fox-Genovese argues, however, that the diary's focus shifted from the individual to society with the advent of the Civil War: "If many [antebellum diaries] function as chronicles of everyday life, most also function as chronicles of personal, intellectual, or spiritual progress. Few women, if any, kept journals primarily to comment upon the society around them. That impulse was born with the Civil War."[35] Steven Kagle classifies nineteenth-century American diaries as belonging to one of two categories: life diaries and situational diaries. As their names suggest, life diaries chronicle an individual's life, while situational diaries are inspired by an event that disrupted an individual life. In the nineteenth-century American South this generally meant travel, courtship, or the most documented episode by diarists in the nineteenth-century South: the Civil War.[36]

With the outbreak of war, Confederate women pursued a greater literary role in society, embarking on new forms of writing in response to the war's manifold challenges. These forms included writing letters and petitions to government officials addressing safety on the home front (as well as the safety of their male relations in the military), writing the Confederate war novel (epitomized in Augusta Jane Evans's *Macaria; or, Altars of Sacrifice*) and smaller patriotic pieces for newspapers and magazines (such as the *Southern Literary Messenger*).[37] In this Confederate culture of self-sacrifice and writing to benefit the common good, "a diary smacked of self-indulgence and self-absorption."[38] As such, diarists were keen to justify writings that seemed to lack a direct link to Confederate service. Butler at times struggled to see the value in her diary in the context of widespread suffering and sacrifice: "I must do [diary writing] no more for I am convinced that this is one great reason why this, above all other production of this genre, is dull and devoid of interest to myself, and I, am sure, would be so to anyone else could they peruse it."[39]

Despite Butler's misgivings about the historical and literary quality of her own diary, the politics of race and gender strikingly penetrate her text in meaningful ways. As a white woman from a slaveholding family, Butler was forced to confront the changing sociopolitical landscape and to find her place in this new world order. At times her statements drew implicit parallels to the American Revolution and the struggle to establish a new republic in the previous century. Other times her statements foreshadowed the southern defeat and the struggle to come to terms with the loss of the southern way of life. Throughout the text Butler is only consistent in her ambiguity: There are both regressive and progressive elements in her views on slavery and gender roles.

Butler's reticence on certain issues is particularly revealing. Her letters make only a single (and brief) reference to slavery by name, and her diary does not mention the institution by name once. In January 1861, after Florida had already seceded and Virginia had yet to do so, and in response to a previous query by her fiancé, she addressed her feelings on the secession crisis: "I can never be a disunionist while I believe that as soon as it is in the power of the South the slave trade will be reopened, an idea which is to me extremely revolting and, apart from the act itself, I feel that the consequences must be in a few years dreadful."[40] She rejected the transatlantic slave trade but not the institution of domestic slavery. This was an argument most closely associated with the political compromise encapsulated in Article 1, Section 9, Clause 1, of the U.S. Constitution brokered by the Founding Fathers in 1787. Although the Confederate Constitution, drafted in March 1861 and ratified in February 1862, prohibited the reopening of the transatlantic slave trade (again, Article 1, Section 9, Clause 1), this was mainly done to promote the prospect of British and French recognition of the Confederacy. Regardless, Butler's expression of concern for the transatlantic slave trade was not indicative of the rest of Butler's narrative. Her diary frequently lists the activities of "servants"—those of her family, her husband, and her neighborhood—without any commentary on the wider political issues surrounding the institution of slavery. Such commentaries reify Suzanne Lebsock's study of antebellum Petersburg women who adopted a "personal frame of reference" (or "personalism") for navigating issues surrounding slavery: White women's daily social interactions with *individual* slaves, especially as workers, better informed their opinions on slavery than political commentaries on the *institution* itself.[41] Like many white southern women of the mid-nineteenth-century South, Butler was more concerned with the tangible reality of interacting with slaves on a daily basis than the abstract justifications (or critiques) of the institution as a whole.[42]

Butler often commented on political issues such as disunion and even her support of John Bell, the Constitutional Union candidate for president in the election of 1860. Yet she was eager to show that while she might have made comments on politics, she was a passive observer, not an active participant, in these masculine affairs. In describing her visit to the Virginia Secession Convention in February 1861, she stated, "I am going to the Convention to be held in Richmond, although I say that I am no politician."[43] A month earlier she elucidated this "apolitical" posturing in a letter to her fiancé: "I have no political opinion, and have a particular dislike to all females who discuss such matters. But I will save my strength for the time of need, and then I will be ready and willing to do everything in my power consistent with my character of a southern lady for the sake of my Country; to deprive myself of every comfort of life and to give life itself; and when that time comes I shall learn what part I ought to play, and I shall perform it, let the dangers be what they may."[44]

Butler rejected a public political voice for herself, and indeed all women, after showcasing her knowledge and ability to engage in such a dialogue and potentially help mold the contemporary political scene. In doing so, she embraced both the rigid doctrine of separate spheres and a sense of female civic virtue: Women could contribute to political culture, albeit within civil society.[45] Furthermore, women could shape public sphere political relations through their private sphere relations with men.[46] In the words of Charlottesville's most famous resident, Thomas

Jefferson, in 1788: "Our good ladies, I trust, have been too wise to wrinkle their foreheads with politics. They are contented to soothe and calm the minds of their husbands returning ruffled from political debate."[47] Likewise, in establishing the new Confederate state, Butler envisioned her role not as a political actor on her own terms but to support male political actors, like her fiancé, and to make sacrifices for her country as required.

While Butler was clearly keen to demonstrate her devotion to the Confederate cause and adherence to antebellum notions of female subservience and docility, there were breakages in this persona. Her frustration with the Confederate war effort and disillusionment with Confederate nationalism is clear after the surrender of Fort Donelson in February 1862.[48] Butler attributed the Union military advancement to Confederate male cowardice: "If I were a man, no such thought would dare enter my mind, but I, being merely a woman, must sit still, with my weak sisters, for fear of doing aught unwomanly, and see 7000 men surrender as they did at Donelson, a deed that women would have blushed to own, and a deed that makes us weep to feel that such men are our countrymen . . . Pure cowardice would be enough to make *men* fight now for if we do not win, what would life be."[49]

She was unequivocal and unapologetic in her indictment of Confederate men for failing to live up to the standards of southern masculinity.[50] She was also astutely aware of the constrictions of her own gender and the disastrous consequences of acting in a way that could be deemed "unwomanly." Her statements on wartime gender roles continually oscillated between the regressive and the progressive. She understood that operating within the boundaries of her gender performed ideological labor for the Confederate republic.[51] Rejecting women's political agency and opinions conformed to expected gender roles and carried out ideological work for the Confederacy. Lambasting the military abilities of its men did not; instead, it actively undermined Confederate nationalism and compromised her contribution of ideological labor to the new state.

In terms of physical labor, the diary shows how southern women were forced to become "mothers of invention" and adopt new labors to ensure the survival of themselves and their families, and hopefully the Confederacy, on the home front.[52] Butler's diary describes a wide range of newly conceived wartime duties, including sewing uniforms, preparing food for nearby encamped soldiers and various efforts to bolster soldiers' spirits. In addition to these descriptions, Butler's diary offers one of the richest and most extended first-person accounts of Confederate home nursing: a subject underdeveloped in the history of Civil War medicine.[53]

The Confederate government mandated the position of nurse in September 1862. Although women had served in nursing capacities from the beginning of the war as volunteers, they only became recognized as professional nurses after the passage of this legislation. In addition to this professionalized labor force, which included celebrated nurses Phoebe Pember Yates and Kate Cumming in its ranks, women also administered in private homes and volunteered in makeshift hospitals to care for wounded soldiers, supplementing the efforts of centralized military hospitals.[54] These women were not paid for their services and found themselves reallocating strained family funds to care for the soldiers. Women who lived closer to battlefields or hospitals were often presented with more opportunities to provide care in their private homes, alleviating stress on the debilitated Confederate Medical Department. Butler's home state of Virginia became an unrelenting battleground. Virginia suffered more battles (122) than any other state during the war, over three times the number of the next state, Tennessee (38). Furthermore, Butler lived close to the Charlottesville General Hospital. The hospital was a series of makeshift buildings around Charlottesville, including the Rotunda at the University of Virginia, which served over twenty-two thousand patients over the course of the war. She became acquainted with the occupation of nursing on family visits to the Charlottesville General Hospital, where she tended to wounded soldiers and at one time had "ten [soldiers] under my charge."[55]

It was from their experiences visiting patients in the overcrowded and chaotic hospital setting that the Wood family felt compelled to extend their services from the hospital into their own home. In August 1861 Lucy Wood Butler's mother had grown increasingly weary of her daughter's prolonged visits to the hospital, fearing for her health and physical safety. Butler's cousin, who also visited the Charlottesville General Hospital, was concerned that one patient in particular, Mr. McIllhaney, would contract typhoid fever if left in the hospital. As a result, Butler was keen to serve as his nurse within her family home. On August 28, 1861, she recorded that he had been "removed here to Charlie's old room upstairs, and, as Mother would not allow me to go to the hospital, I have been the nurse of this young man. He is so gentle and amiable that it is a pleasure to attend to his wants."[56]

Home nursing was not just physical labor but also ideological labor for the new republic. Perhaps best exemplified in Augusta Jane Evans's best-selling wartime novel *Macaria; or, Altars of Sacrifice* (1864), nursing was valorized as southern women's self-sacrificing service to the republic. There was no better way for a woman to demonstrate her devotion to the Confederacy than through nursing. In this way nursing, in both the public and private spheres, physically and ideologically contributed to the war effort. Home nursing was absolutely central to the sustainability of the southern war effort in the context of a chaotic and inefficient Confederate Medical Department: Butler's diary can be read as one woman's experience of the causes, course, and consequences of wartime nursing within the private sphere.

Lucy Wood Butler's diary offers an ordinary perspective on an extraordinary event. Through the union of Waddy Butler and Lucy Wood and the disunion of the United States, the narrative of the newborn project of the Confederacy takes shape and reveals the crucial interplay between "history from above" and "history from below." Exceptional men, leading exceptional states, fighting exceptional battles is only half the story of the American Civil War. The other half is how the war was actually experienced and challenged in ordinary lives, and that story is just as important.

NOTES

1. Charles (b. 1836), Elizabeth (b. 1839), Lucy (b. 1841), Lydia (b. 1843), Alfred (b. 1845), Snowden (b. 1847), Walter (b. 1849), and Lewis (b. 1855). Maria (1853) and Benjamin (1862–69) died in childhood.

2. For more on Charlottesville in the Civil War, see Ervin L. Jordan Jr., *Charlottesville and the University of Virginia in the Civil War* (Lynchburg, Va.: H. E. Howard, 1988); and Ervin L. Jordan Jr. and Herbert A. Thomas Jr., *19th Virginia Infantry* (Lynchburg, Va.: H. E. Howard, 1987).

3. Henry Clay, letter to John Wood Jr., September 10, 1846, Albert and Shirley Smalls Special Collections Library, University of Virginia, Charlottesville.

4. For more on Confederate courtship, see Anya Jabour, "'Days of Lightly-Won and Lightly-Held Hearts': Courtship and Coquetry in the Southern Confederacy," in *Weirding the War: Stories from the Civil War's Ragged Edges,* ed. Stephen Berry (Athens: University of Georgia Press, 2011), 95–121. For more on antebellum South courtship, see Anya Jabour, *Scarlett's Sisters: Young Women in the Old South* (Chapel Hill: University of North Carolina Press, 2007), 113–80.

5. October 12, 1860.

6. By mid-1862 the Second Florida Regiment would join the Army of Northern Virginia.

7. From this point Lucy Wood will be referred to as Lucy Butler given her recent marriage and subsequent change of surname.

8. July 1861 (entry does not include day).

9. May 24, 1861.

10. December 26, 1862.

11. May 7, 1861 (Milton) and June 15, 1861 (Byron). See note 33 in the introduction for more information on southern women's education.

12. March 19, 1863.

13. In April 1861 the Charlottesville and University Battalion was formed. In May 1861 the 19th Virginia Regiment was formed; it was composed of many Charlottesville area men. Again, for more information on Charlottesville in the war, see Jordan, *Charlottesville and the University of Virginia;* and Jordan and Thomas, *19th Virginia Infantry.*

14. Butler had been promoted to the rank of first lieutenant by the time of his death.

15. July 3, 1863.

16. William Gilmore Simms, letter to Lucy Wood Butler, January 13, 1865, Albert and Shirley Smalls Special Collections Library, UVA.

17. George T. Brown, letter to Lucy Wood Butler, box 2, Fishburne Family Papers, Albert and Shirley Smalls Special Collections Library, UVA.

18. Boxes 2–4, Fishburne Family Papers, UVA.

19. Lucy Wood Butler, letter to Eliza Harper Wood, October 1876, box 3, Fishburne Family Papers. This was a much more moderate expedition than those embarked upon by other southern women, such as Sarah Dawson Morgan, who traveled to Europe after the war for a version of the Grand Tour, UVA.

20. Lucy Wood Butler Correspondence, box 4, Fishburne Family Papers, UVA.

21. Beverly Smith, "Idyllic Ivy," *Danville Register,* February 19, 1930, box 5, Fishburne Family Papers. Smith claimed to have lived in Ivy sporadically between 1910 and 1914, UVA.

22. For the classic studies of women in the slaveholding class on the eve of the Civil War, see Catherine Clinton, *The Plantation Mistress: Woman's World in the Old South* (New York: Pantheon, 1982); Elizabeth Fox-Genovese, *Within the Plantation Household: Black and White Women of the Old South* (Chapel Hill: University of North Carolina Press, 1988); Jean E. Friedman, *The Enclosed Garden: Women and Community in the Evangelical South, 1830–1900* (Chapel Hill: University of North Carolina Press, 1985); and Anne Firor Scott, *The Southern Lady: From Pedestal to Politics, 1830–1930* (Chicago: University of Chicago Press, 1970).

23. Mary Boykin Chesnut, *A Diary from Dixie,* ed. Isabella Martin and Myrta Lockett Avary (New York: D. Appleton, 1905); Mary Boykin Chesnut, *A Diary from Dixie,* ed. Ben Ames Williams (Boston: Houghton Mifflin, 1949); Mary Boykin Chesnut, *Mary Chesnut's Civil War,* ed. C. Vann Woodward (New Haven, Conn.: Yale University Press, 1981); and Mary Boykin Chesnut, *The Private Mary Chesnut: The Unpublished Civil War Diaries,* ed. C. Vann Woodward and Elisabeth Muhlenfeld (New York: Oxford University Press, 1984).

24. Judith White McGuire, *Diary of a Southern Refugee during the War, by a Lady of Virginia,* ed. Jean V. Berlin (Lincoln: University of Nebraska Press, 1995), intro., esp. xiii.

25. Chesnut, *Diary from Dixie,* 20.

26. Abraham Lincoln, "First Inaugural Address: March 4, 1861," The Avalon Project: Documents in Law, History and Diplomacy, Yale Law School.

27. Abraham Lincoln, "House Divided Speech: June 16, 1858," Gilder Lehrman Institute of American History.

28. March 3, 1863.

29. Given that the text is typescript and the prose is clear and concise, it is very likely that Lucy Wood Butler's diary underwent at least minor editorial changes after the war. Still, these editorial changes were not completed for commercial publication with a commercial editor (as in the case of Mary Chesnut). For more on editorial changes to the diary, see "Note on the Text."

30. Amy L. Wink, *She Left Nothing in Particular: The Autobiographical Legacy of Nineteenth-Century Women's Diaries* (Knoxville: University of Tennessee Press, 2001), intro.

31. Giselle Roberts, *The Confederate Belle* (Columbia: University of Missouri Press, 2003), 23.

32. For more on the classics in antebellum education, see Carl J. Richard, *The Golden Age of the Classics in America: Greece, Rome and the Antebellum United States* (Cambridge: Harvard University Press, 2009), 7–9. For more on women's informal and formal education in the classics, see Caroline Winterer, *Mirror of*

Antiquity: American Women and the Classical Tradition, 1750–1900 (Cornell, N.Y.: Cornell University Press, 2007).

33. For additional information on southern women's antebellum education, see Christie Farnham, *The Education of the Southern Belle: Higher Education and Student Socialization in the Antebellum South* (New York: New York University Press, 1994); Mary Kelly, *Learning to Stand and Speak: Women, Education and Public Life in America's Republic* (Chapel Hill: University of North Carolina Press, 2008), esp. 34–111; Victoria E. Ott, *Confederate Daughters: Coming of Age during the Civil War* (Carbondale: Southern Illinois University Press, 2008), 15–26; and Jabour, *Scarlett's Sisters,* 47–82.

34. Roberts, *Confederate Belle,* 11.

35. Fox-Genovese, *Within the Plantation Household,* 252.

36. Steven Kagle, *Early Nineteenth-Century American Diary Literature* (Boston: Twayne, 1986), 2.

37. For an extended discussion of southern women's literary contributions to Confederate society, see Drew Gilpin Faust, *Mothers of Invention: Women of the Slaveholding South in the American Civil War* (Chapel Hill: University of North Carolina Press, 1996), esp. 162.

38. Faust, *Mothers of Invention,* 163.

39. November 27, 1862. Suzanne Bunkers, "Reading and Interpreting Unpublished Diaries by Nineteenth-Century Women," *a/b: Auto/Biography Studies* 2 (1986): 15. For more information on the life and literary processes of diaries, see Ellen Gruber Garvey, "Anonymity, Authorship, and Recirculation: A Civil War Episode," *Book History* 9 (2006): 159–78.

40. January 21, 1861.

41. Suzanne Lebsock, *The Free Women of Petersburg: Status and Culture in a Southern Town, 1784–1860* (New York: Norton, 1984), 138–41.

42. For more on the intellectual history of proslavery thought in the Old South, see Drew Gilpin Faust, ed., *The Ideology of Slavery: Proslavery Thought in the Antebellum South, 1830–1860* (Baton Rouge: Louisiana State University Press, 1981); Eugene Genovese, *The Slaveholder's Dilemma: Freedom and Progress in Southern Conservative Thought, 1820–1860* (Columbia: University of South Carolina Press, 1992); and Michael O'Brien, *Placing the South* (Jackson: University Press of Mississippi, 2007), sec. 2.

43. February 11, 1861.

44. January 21, 1861.

45. See Elizabeth R. Varon, *We Mean to Be Counted: White Women and Politics in Antebellum Virginia* (Chapel Hill: University of North Carolina Press, 1998).

46. For more on women's politics in early America, see Linda Kerber, *Women of the Republic: Intellect and Ideology in Revolutionary America* (Chapel Hill: University of North Carolina Press, 1980); Mary Beth Norton, *Liberty's Daughters: The Revolutionary Experience of American Women, 1750–1800* (Boston: Little, Brown, 1980); and Rosemarie Zagarri, *Revolutionary Backlash: Women and Politics in the Early Republic* (Philadelphia: University of Pennsylvania Press, 2007).

47. Thomas Jefferson, *Jefferson: Political Writings,* ed. Joyce Appleby and Terence Ball (Cambridge: Cambridge University Press, 1999), letter to Anne Willing Bingham, May 11, 1788, 543.

48. For more on Confederate nationalism, see Drew Gilpin Faust, *The Creation of Confederate Nationalism: Ideology and Identity in the Civil War South* (Baton Rouge: Louisiana State University Press, 1988); Stephanie McCurry, *Confederate Reckoning: Power and Politics in the Civil War South* (Cambridge: Harvard University Press, 2010); James McPherson, *For Cause and Comrades: Why Men Fought in the Civil War* (Oxford: Oxford University Press, 1999), and *What They Fought For, 1861–1865* (Baton Rouge: Louisiana State University Press, 1994); Eric Foner, *Politics and Ideology in the Age of the Civil War* (Oxford: Oxford University Press, 1980); George Rable, *Civil Wars: Women and the Crisis of Southern Nationalism* (Urbana: University of Illinois Press, 1989); and Gary W. Gallagher, *The Confederate War* (Cambridge: Harvard University Press, 1999).

49. February 27, 1862.

50. For more on southern masculinity, see Stephen W. Berry, *All That Makes a Man: Love and Ambition in the Civil War South* (Oxford: Oxford University Press, 2003); Lorri Glover, *Southern Sons: Becoming Men in the New Nation* (Baltimore, Md.: Johns Hopkins University Press, 2007); Craig Thompson Friend and Lorri Glover, eds., *Southern Manhood: Perspectives on Masculinity in the Old South* (Athens: University of Georgia Press, 2004); Amy Murrell Taylor, *Divided Family in Civil War America* (Chapel Hill: University of North Carolina Press, 2005); and Kenneth Noe, *Reluctant Rebels: The Confederates Who Joined the Army after 1861* (Chapel Hill: University of North Carolina Press, 2015).

51. For more on Confederate gender relations and roles, see LeeAnn Whites and Alecia P. Long, eds., *Occupied Women: Gender, Military Occupation, and the American Civil War* (Baton Rouge: Louisiana State University Press, 2009); LeeAnn Whites, *The Civil War as a Crisis in Gender: Augusta, Georgia, 1860–1890* (Athens: University of Georgia Press, 1995); Catherine Clinton and Nina Silber, eds., *Divided Houses: Gender and the Civil War* (Oxford: Oxford University Press, 1992); Nina Silber, *Gender and the Sectional Conflict* (Chapel Hill: University of North Carolina Press, 2008); and Bertram Wyatt-Brown, *The Shaping of South-*

ern Culture: Honor, Grace, and War, 1760s–1880s (Chapel Hill: University of North Carolina Press, 2001).

52. See Faust, *Mothers of Invention.* As Faust focuses on elite women, Butler's diary shows the extension of Faust's assertions into the more middling classes.

53. For more on the Confederate Medical Department and nursing, see H. H. Cunningham, *Doctors in Gray: The Confederate Medical Service* (Baton Rouge: Louisiana State University Press, 1958); Carol C. Green, *Chimborazo: The Confederacy's Largest Hospital* (Knoxville: University of Tennessee Press, 2004); and Libra R. Hilde, *Worth a Dozen Men: Women and Nursing in the Civil War South* (Charlottesville: University of Virginia Press, 2012). In particular, see Jane E. Schultz, *Women at the Front: Hospital Workers in Civil War America* (Chapel Hill: University of North Carolina Press, 2004). There are somewhat reliable statistics estimating the number of women serving as Union nurses (21,208 according to the Carded Service Records). Given the burning of Richmond in 1865 (including the Confederacy's medical records) and the number of southern women engaged in home or private nursing projects, there is no firm calculation of the number of women who served as Confederate nurses (Schultz, *Women at the Front,* 21).

54. For accounts of Confederate hospital nursing, see Phoebe Yates Pember, *A Southern Woman's Story: Life in Confederate Richmond,* ed. Bell Irvin Wiley, 2nd ed. (Atlanta: Mockingbird Books, 1974); Kate Cumming, *The Journal of Kate Cumming: A Confederate Nurse, 1862–1865,* ed. R. Harwell, 2nd ed. (Savannah: Beehive Press, 1975); and Ada Bacot, *A Confederate Nurse: The Diary of Ada W. Bacot, 1860–1863,* ed. Jean V. Berlin (Columbia: University of South Carolina Press, 1994). There are multiple published editions of the Pember and Cumming journals.

55. July 19, 1861.

56. August 28, 1861.

Letters of
LUCY WOOD and WADDY BUTLER
(May 1859–May 1861)

Virginia. May 22, 1859

Miss Lucy,

Will you give me the great pleasure of permitting me to accompany you to church this evening at half past eight?

Respectfully,
Waddy Butler

Virginia. May 16, 1860

Dear Lucy,

I have fortunately secured a horse that is at least respectable; and I will come for you about half past four to take the ride to Farmington.[1]

If Miss Maggie has come, she would perhaps like to ride with us.[2]

Yours affect,
Waddy Butler

The Grove (Florida). July 4, 1860

Dearest Lucy,

Here I am writing my fourth letter to you, whilst from you I have received only one.

1. Farmington is located just outside of Charlottesville, to the west, and to the east of Ivy.
2. According to a footnote in the original text, Maggie was a distant cousin of Lucy Wood.

Have you forgotten your promise so very soon, or has one of those unfortunate contingencies, which you foretold, arisen to prevent a compliance?

Perhaps I am wrong in imputing any failure on your part, and it may be that the fault consists in some disarrangement in the mail. Be it as it may, I have been most grievously disappointed.

I am leading an idle listless life here in Florida; yet, strange as it may appear, a very pleasant one.

I spent the entire day in the house, eating fruit, reading only such books as cater to my indolent humor, discussing some subject that requires little mental exertion with my guardian who is an agreeable companion in hot weather, lying on my back smoking "the vile weed," and lastly dreaming of a little fairy far away in the Old Dominion.[3]

I have gradually recovered from those sad feelings which commenced with my departure from Virginia, and in their place have come others of more sanguine hue. Instead of uselessly repining, I have made firm determinations. Although the future for me is somewhat clouded, yet the *couleur de rose* is in the predominant. With you I shall be content; and that is the height of human happiness.

At the beginning of next month I shall enter the office of some lawyer where I will remain until I arrive at the man's estate—which very important event will happen next February—and then I will commence the practice of my profession in some favourable locality, perhaps at Pensacola. Toward the close of the aforementioned year, I'll come for my betrothed; and then the future may take care of itself, for I shall not regard it with the least anxiety.

I have written you an insipid letter, my darling. Ascribe it to the hot weather and not to any fault of mine.

May God bless you, dearest.

Your lover,
Waddy Butler

3. The "vile weed" refers to tobacco.

Charlottesville (Virginia). July 28, 1860

Dear Waddy,

When I last heard from you, you had just returned from St. Augustine where you had been enjoying the delightful society of a charming Spanish girl, together with fine fruits and sea bathing.

This presents quite a different contrast to my pastimes and enjoyments for we have had so much dry weather that we have no fruit, and then both of my sisters have gone with all of my friends to the country, but I have enjoyed the solitude, and I have been reading some very interesting books, and then I have the delightful amusement of teaching my littler brother.

Maggie returned to Washington yesterday. I went to the country the day before to bid her goodbye. She seemed very sorry to leave us, but as she expected to meet one of her friends from the South at home, I think that his society will soon dissipate all feelings of sadness.

I suppose that you are now in Fernandina, and have commenced or rather resumed your very "hard studying," which I expect is not very agreeable after having had your time at your own disposal for so long, and then I expect that you are frequently interrupted by dreams of the pretty Spanish Girl.

Mr. King called a week or two ago much to our surprise for he professed to be going home when we saw him last, but he had just returned from Caperton's, and seemed very much pleased with his visit so I think it must have been a successful one, for he told us that he would not return to the University but expected to see us frequently.

You must tell me if your eldest Brother has married the lady you were telling me of, and you must let me know what became of Mr. Nick Butler.[4]

I suppose my third letter will not reach you at all as you will have left your home before its arrival, and I expect this will share the same fate so it is useless for me to write more.

Yours very truly,
Lucy Wood

4. Nick Butler was Waddy's brother.

Charlottesville. August 11, 1860

Dear Waddy,

I received your letter a few days since and although I considered it of sufficient importance to be answered immediately I thought it best to take your advice and first well consider the matter.[5]

Not that I required time to decide whether I should forsake you now that misfortunes have come, or whether or not I could endure a life of poverty for I have both good health and energy which would constitute a sufficient fortune for me, even were you utterly penniless, provided your feelings remained unchanged.

But besides this there were many things in your letter that made me doubt what course I should pursue.

You sayed that you would not be able to maintain the same position in society which you now have. This would indeed be a very great sacrifice for you to make and I beg you to tell me if you are willing, if you can make it; but if your love is too weak to stand the test then tell me so, for if this is the case it is not worth having.

When I first read your letter I was prompted to return a very different answer from this for I thought you could mean nothing but to intimate that you were ready and willing to renounce all claims to my heart and hand but I am slow to take hints, and if such was your meaning you must speak still plainer, for I concluded that if such had been your meaning you would surely not have commenced your letter with a reproof, and then I place too much confidence in you to think, or rather to believe, that you would have adopted such means as these if you had

5. There is a note in Wood's papers that summarizes the previous letter from Waddy Butler: "Fernandina, August 5, 1860. Misgivings. Money wasted, not twenty-five but twelve hundred a year." The full text of this letter is not in her papers. Although this is a complete record of the letters exchanged between Lucy Wood and Waddy Butler present in Lucy Wood's papers at the Virginia Historical Society, University of Virginia, and University of North Carolina–Chapel Hill, this is an incomplete record of all of the letters actually exchanged between Lucy Wood and Waddy Butler between 1859 and 1861. At times a letter from Waddy Butler is missing in the exchange; other times a letter from Lucy Wood is missing in the exchange. For more on the editorship of the letters and diary, see "Note on the Text."

been weary of this engagement, especially since you have promised to tell me plainly wherever you are.

I regret very much that you have been so unfortunate, and I know how much it will sadden you when you find it necessary to give up many luxuries, and find that you cannot gratify every wish, but you should not allow yourself to be grieved by such things, and I doubt that it will prove a blessing and that you will go forth from the trying ordeal a wiser and better man.

With much love I remain,
Yours Lucy Wood

Locust Hill (Virginia). August 25, 1860

Dearest Waddy,

Your most welcome though sad letter reached me today after having been detained several days in the office, for I am now visiting my friends in the country.[6] I am very sorry to hear of your being in so much distress and in such bad health, but I hope that by this time both you and your brother have recovered, and if such is the case I know of nothing that should any longer make you unhappy.

It is true that your ideas of wealth have been suddenly dissipated, and yet still you are far from being reduced to poverty as you seem to imagine. Of course, such an income as yours will require very plain living, but not a life destitute of comfort or requiring great hardships.

September 3rd. I was obliged to stop here for fear of intruding on Sunday, and I was so busy during the rest of my visit preparing little Mollie Anderson to return home with me and to school that I could not find time to finish my letter, but hoped to do so on Saturday when I returned home, but I had such a violent headache then that it was impossible for me to sit up.[7]

I have just read your letter to Lizzie and I am much obliged to you for

6. There is a note in her papers that summarizes the previous letter from Waddy Butler: "Fernandina, August 18th/1860. Illness of his brother. His own poor health and depression." The full text of the letter is not in her papers.

7. Wood often taught and cared for Anderson, her cousin.

the beautiful little compliment you payed me in comparing me to stiff, hard soil, but perhaps I have been too hasty in applying this to myself, for you may have been referring to some other correspondent.[8]

I was very happy to see that you wrote in much better spirits and that you had regained your health and I suppose that your brother has now recovered also.

Maggie writes quite frequently and she always inquires after you, and in her last letter she sayed that she did not believe you had ever liked her really, or you would not have forgotten her so soon, and she takes it for granted that this is the case by your never sending her any messages, but I feel very sure she is mistaken. I hope so at any rate for I love her so much that I would not like for you not to have the same feeling toward her.

Charlie returned a few days since from the North after a visit of two weeks.[9] He saw Lizzie Benton several times, but he says that her health is so bad that she has lost all of her beauty.

Every one here seems to be in a state of excitement on account of a marriage that they think will take place very soon, that of Miss Nannie Carrington and Howe Cochran, but the people here are so much interested in such matters that they are apt to be a little hasty in their conclusions.

It grows late and as I have to write Maggie now, I must bid you good night. Please answer this soon.

Yours in love,
Lucy Wood

Fernandina (Florida). September 8, 1860

Dearest Lucy,

Your kind affectionate letter came today, and a most welcome letter it was. I had, only this morning, written to you; and I formed all kinds of conjectures about your long silence. I am very glad that my surmises have proved incorrect. I have no desire of being a true prophet when I prophesize concerning disasters and annoyances.

I am happy to tell you that my brother has recovered after having

8. Lizzie was Lucy Wood's older sister (Elizabeth, b. 1839).

9. Charlie was Lucy Wood's older brother (Charles, b. 1836).

been on the verge of the grave struggling with death. He is still very weak and feeble; and his constitution is seriously injured, I fear past all recovery. My late illness proceeded, I suppose, as much from mental anxiety as from any physical cause, for as soon as my brother began to mend I got well. I am now enjoying my usual health and spirits, neither of which, however, are exuberant.

You say truly that I have nothing to make me unhappy, nothing to cause the unmanly weakness and pitiful despair which at times overcome me. My friends are kind, my relatives affectionate, my fortune at least amounts to a competency, I have brains sufficient to prevent being classed with fools, and I possess your love. What more could I desire, what else could add to my happiness! Well I occasionally am as happy as a mortal can well be, then I suffer a relapse into the old feeling of gloom and melancholy, I become discontented and restless, dissatisfied with myself and hating the world, wishing for what I know not what. It is foolish and silly I know; and I strive to overcome this great weakness of my mind with all my might and endeavor. Your love, dear Lucy, will, I trust, prove the means of my regeneration.

Do make this apology to Miss Maggie for me: I did not know you were her correspondent, and in what manner my messages could reach their destination. Tell her that I would very much prefer sending my own messages, that is, with her assent.

What think you, I have begun to be a politician, yes *mirabile dictu.* I have delivered a political speech before the citizens of Fernandina and doubtless I shall deliver many more before the close of the present Presidential campaign. Nick too has turned politician, and is canvassing the State with the democratic candidate for governor.[10] My maiden speech threatened to be a miserable failure, for when I rose, my consciousness and my speech along with it fell, and no doubt I said some foolish things, but gradually I regained confidence and self-possession, and then, I believe, acquitted myself pretty well. I have now broken the ice, and conquered the greatest difficulty.

10. The Democratic candidate for governor of Florida in the 1860 election was John Milton. He won the election and served as Florida's governor from October 1861 to April 1865, when he committed suicide.

Tell Miss Lizzie I am anxiously awaiting her reply to my letter.

Good night, sweet love.

Your lover,
Waddy Butler

Fernandina. September 29, 1860

Dearest Lucy,

I returned only yesterday after an absence of a week's duration, attending my brother's wedding, and I found your letter waiting for me in the post.

I enjoyed myself exceedingly at the wedding and I think every one did, and I do not recollect of ever having spent an evening more pleasantly. The number of guests was not large, yet large enough to make the party a gay one, there was a good supper, excellent wine, and well-bred agreeable people. The bride, whose name—I believe I have not told you—is Caroline Floyd, is a most beautiful girl; and her beauty on the evening of her wedding was as perfect as I have ever seen.

I officiated as one of the groomsmen. On the morning after the marriage the happy couple left for a trip, and the remainder of us staid behind to celebrate their nuptials for a week longer.

My dear Lucy I am very grateful for your well-intended advice, and if I lived in Virginia would follow it, but here it is wholly inapplicable where every man, *nolens aut volens,* is forced to take a most active part in politics, and if he does not is regarded as a numskull. I assure it is foreign both to my wishes and inclinations to make speeches of any sort more especially political ones, but when I am appointed to deliver a speech I cannot act otherwise than to try my best.

I am becoming very impatient for our marriage for I am wearied, tired at times almost to madness, of my present mode of life; I long for a home of my own and some one, to whom I can give my whole confidence and my whole heart, to preside over it. I almost despair when I consider the length of time that must elapse before you and I be united, yet I trust it may be sooner than now seems possible.

If I ask your hand, to be given me in holy wedlock next March, will you say me nay? Then I shall be a man, legally my own master, and be able to offer you a home, poor though it may be.

If my little income is not sufficient, my capital is large enough to support us decently until my practice shall become remunerative.

Many people have married with less, have lived contented, and died happy.

You and I may and can do likewise. Let us get married, go to some place where we know no one, live quietly and economically, and strive to be contented. If we do this, I think as much happiness as usually falls to the lot of mortals will be ours.

Your lover,
Waddy Butler

Charlottesville. October 12, 1860

My dear Waddy,

Your long expected letter was most welcomely received on Tuesday last when I had just concluded to wait no longer for a letter from you but to write immediately and ask the reason of your silence, for I feared that you had been ill, and was happy to hear that you had been enjoying yourself from home.

I fear you quite envied your happy brother his beautiful Bride, when you thought of the homely ill-natured little creature that may one day be your bride.

I think that you did not suspect me of interested motives when I expressed my dislike for your becoming a politician for I had no doubt that all of your sympathies were with your native State, while I am very much interested in Mr. Bell; as the ladies have been exhorted to exert their influence with the Gentlemen for him, you must excuse me for attempting it in an indirect manner, by trying to silence so formidable an opponent as yourself.[11]

One reason that I have not answered your last letter sooner is that I wished to decide what answer I had best make to the question which you propounded to me.

11. Former Tennessee congressman (1827–41) and senator (1847–59) as well as secretary of war (1841) John Bell was the Constitutional Union Party's candidate in the 1860 presidential election in which Abraham Lincoln claimed victory. Bell finished third in the election. He carried three states (Kentucky, Tennessee, and Virginia), thirty-nine electoral votes, and 12.6 percent of the popular vote.

I know of no objection to your proposal except I think it would be much better for you to first choose your home wherever you may think best (for it is a matter of indifference to me where that may be) and to commence business, but of course you know much more of such matters than I do, and if you still prefer it, I will willingly accede to your wishes. But I feel so sure that a great calamity will ere long befall us and our country that I dread the idea of making plans for the future.

I fear you will think I am in a melancholy mood, but when I tell you that the Charlottesville band is playing, the soldiers marching, and an opera troupe practising very near me, besides my protégée, little Mary Anderson, running in and talking to me, I do not think that you will be at all surprised.[12]

Maggie sends her kind regards, and says that if she is to understand from your message that you wish a correspondence with her, she is sorry that she cannot comply with your request, but her mother positively objects to her corresponding with Gentlemen except under peculiar circumstances, and as she cannot state the present circumstances to her Mother she finds it impossible to write. Miss Kate Stockton has been inquiring after your Brother Nick. I suppose it is because he has recently shown so much interest in her.

Excuse me for not writing more as I have promised to walk in the country with the children.

Yours truly,
Lucy Wood

Fernandina. December 14, 1860

Dearest Lucy,

Your letter came yesterday, and though very brief yet it was most comforting.[13]

12. Mary Anderson was referred to as Mollie Anderson in Wood's earlier letter dated August 25.

13. There is a note in her papers that summarizes the previous letter from Waddy Butler: "Fernandina, Nov. 14, 1860. Death of brother, William, in N.C. on wedding tour." The full text of this letter, or her response, is not in her papers.

I would to God that your hopes, your advice, your admonitions could be realized—that my heart was prepared to feel the influence of the Holy Spirit—that my mind was comforted and cheered by divine religion—that my soul was ready to meet death and to meet God.

I clearly recognize the power and energy of God in the conversion of my dear brother. I have prayed God to pardon my sins and give me "grace unto repentance." I have read the Bible with a sincere spirit and an earnest desire of comprehending its great truths, and yet my soul is still full of sin and wickedness.

I trust that I may have strength to continue to seek after Christ until I shall at last find him.

Florida is in a state of active preparation for secession—a convention has been called to sit on the 3rd of Jan. next, and it will, beyond the shadow of a doubt, determine upon immediate secession.[14]

The State has not only made a liberal appropriation by its legislature for the purchasing of arms, but the people also are freely contributing their money for the same purpose. Every man, woman and child in the State desire secession, and are perfectly willing to fight in the "cause."

I heard of an old lady, living on this island, who said she would "first send her sons to fight the Yankees and when they were killed she would go herself."

We are anxious for a bout with the North, and I believe we shall not be disappointed. I have already told you, I think, that I am the first lieutenant of an infantry company. We offered our services to the governor, and if there is any service to be performed we will be ordered out among the first. I shall rejoice beyond all measure should there arise an opportunity of revenging some of the injuries and insults received by the South at the hands of the North. Should that opportunity ever come the Southern people will give their "brethren" good cause to remember the day.

I shall spend my Christmas at home, and I only wish that you may enjoy yours as quietly and pleasantly as I anticipate for myself.

14. On January 10, 1861, delegates in Tallahassee voted for Florida to secede from the Union.

The only present I ask from you is a long and loving letter. I will send you some little thing to remind you that I am still in the land of the living.

Your loving Waddy

Charlottesville. January 21, 1861

My Dear Waddy,

You cannot realize how very happy I was on receiving your letter on the 19th for I had been looking for it for such a long, long time, and had at last given up in despair of hearing from you, and though it was not a very cheering letter, yet it raised my spirits very much; but I am even willing to be deprived of the pleasure of hearing from you as often as I otherwise should when I know that your time is occupied in the services of your country, though we are foreigners to each other now, but I do not doubt but that yours will soon be the common cause with us, and that Virginia will be united with the South by the bond of disunion, for secession is fast becoming the order of the day here.

I feel very sorry for you Southerners who have been raised to consider any kind of manual labor a degradation. It will be so hard to become used to the hardships of war, and you seem already to have had some bitter, or rather, severe, experience.

It is sayed of Mr. Earle that he intends going to battle in his carriage and ordering his servants to shoot those Yankees, but not to make a noise—he is nervous.

But it is sayed that he will marry my pretty cousin, Betty Price, soon, as he still remains here I suppose he thinks that South Carolina can spare him better than Miss Price.

Mother has been sick for some time past, though even sickness cannot quench her patriotic zeal, for she has been giving vent to her feelings by slight effusions in our paper which very much exasperates the ladies as she gives them a little advice and recommends economy until the crisis is over.

I have been housekeeping ever since Christmas and entertaining visitors, until a week since, when I had to resign all other duties and devote my attention to myself, for, owing to my size, the mumps mistook me for a child, and I am just recovering from it.

You wished to know if I had changed my opinion on the disunion question. Well, to some extent I have, yet I can never be a disunionist while I believe that as soon as it is in the power of the South the slave trade will be reopened, an idea which is to me extremely revolting and, apart from the act itself, I feel that the consequences must be in a few years dreadful.

But I have no political opinion, and have a particular dislike to all females who discuss such matters. But I will save my strength for the time of need, and then I will be ready and willing to do everything in my power consistent with my character of a southern lady for the sake of my Country; to deprive myself of every comfort of life and to give life itself; and when that time comes I shall learn what part I ought to play, and I shall perform it, let the dangers be what they may.

It is my sincere hope and prayer that you may pass safely through the dangers that must soon surround you, and that you will, as I know you must, acquit yourself nobly, but O! do not forget in excitement and turmoil your Creator and your Saviour.

Whenever you come you will be most welcome, and I will know how to account for it if I do not hear from you often.

With much love I remain yours truly,

L.W.

Fernandina. January 31, 1861

Dearest Lucy,

Your letter came yesterday, and almost contrary to my expectation; for I had believed that the government had ceased to convey the mails through South Carolina.[15]

You must never expect very cheering or cheerful letters from me: I am unable to write them. There is not a particle either of wit or humor in my composition. My disposition is a sour, morose, and discontented

15. On December 20, 1860, the South Carolina convention voted unanimously to adopt an ordinance to dissolve the connection between the United States and South Carolina. South Carolina was the first state to secede from the Union.

one. I regret that I am so unfortunately constituted, as much for your sake as for my own.

I am not surprised at the rapid spread of the doctrine of secession in Virginia.

The folly of the administration, and the fanaticism of the Republican party, will force every Southern State from the present Union into the Southern Confederacy.

But a truce to politics: I am writing a letter to my sweetheart, and not an article for the newspapers.

What a brave patriotic girl you are! I am sure you would act as nobly as you speak. I am very proud of possessing the love of one so courageous.

I shall be admitted to the practice of law about the first of March, and then, if not engaged in fighting the Yankees, I will go to Pensacola on a prospecting tour. If I like the place and society, and if there appears to be a likelihood for me of obtaining a practice, I will determine to live there. Should the formed surmises end in accordance with my wishes, I will then come to Virginia and bring you to your new home.

I wish you would write me—on behalf of Nick—whether Miss Stockton and Glover have yet been united in the "holy bonds of matrimony." The announcement of their engagement very much astonished me; for I believed that he was not at all a favorite. However, her end has been like that of all flirts: to marry fools or rascals. I am sorry for Miss Kate, that it is her fate to be linked for life to such a fellow as Glover.

I hinted in my last letter to Miss Lizzie that I would perhaps be present at the attack on the Pensacola forts; but, to my deep regret and chagrin, my company has been ordered to remain at this place, where I shall probably see no fighting for two months to come.[16] I expected confidently to entertain you in my next letter with a narration of my first battle, of hair-breadth escapes and desperate adventures; but my

16. Butler joined the Second Florida Infantry on July 13, 1861, as an adjutant.

foolish governor has disappointed me, and consequently I am compelled to disappoint you.

In love I am yours,
W. B. Butler

Charlottesville. February 11, 1861

My Dear Waddy,

I received your letter a few hours since and now hasten to answer it, as I shall leave home in the morning, for I am going to the Convention to be held in Richmond, although I say that I am no politician; and expect to spend a week or two with my friend, Miss Street.[17]

I am sorry to hear that your spirits are so low, but do not regret the cause at all. I am afraid that you will soon be gratified in your desire for fighting, but you seem to have forgotten the possibility of not making the hairbreadth escapes, and then the news I would have from you might not be so agreeable to me as you imagine it will be.

I was speaking a few days since of the plans to which you referred in your last letter, but Mother told me that she could never give her consent to my going South in the spring or summer as she fears for my health.

Now I am very sorry that I could not have told you this before; but this was the first time I had mentioned the subject and had no idea that these objections would be raised.

But notwithstanding I hope it will not be long before I see you again for it has been a long, very long while since you went away.

I hope the Governor will continue as kind and considerate as he has been so far.

17. The Virginia Convention of 1861 convened in Richmond with 152 delegates on February 13. At the beginning the delegation expressed strong Unionist support and on April 4 voted against secession. See n. 20 in "Letters" for information on the April 17 convention vote, after the Battle of Fort Sumter and Lincoln's call for seventy-five thousand volunteers.

I wish I could write more and could say a great deal that I cannot express, but I find it impossible to do so.

I had nearly forgotten to tell you of Miss Stockton, and I cannot now answer your question as to whether she has married Mr. Glover or not, but still continues to live at her house.

Good Night. I am very truly yours with much love, Lucy.

Fernandina. February 20, 1861.

Dearest Lucy,

After a long weary time of waiting, your letter has come. Do for heaven's sake write more punctually and at greater length.

Your letters give me more pleasure than it is possible for me to derive from any other source. It would be an easy task for you to add to my pleasure by making an addition to the length of your letters.

I am not surprised that Mrs. Wood has made objections to your coming South in the spring or summer. You Virginians regard the climate of Florida with the utmost horror, you hold the same estimate of it that the English do of India, and you believe that every unacclimated person, coming here during the warm season, must necessarily die.

Now I can warrant you that this belief is unfounded and wholly mistaken. The climate of Florida is not only more healthy but it is also more pleasant than that of Virginia.

However, if she is unwilling that you should come, I shall resign myself to wait as patiently as may be until next fall.

In reading your letter I was struck with a particular sentence. What your words express is most true, and I am sad, most sad, that it is true. The sentence is this: "I wish I could write more, and I would say a great deal that I cannot express, but I find it impossible to do so."

Yes, Lucy, through loving me you "find it impossible" to talk to me in the language of love. You have been writing to me such plain matter-of-fact letters so long that the habit has become as invincible as nature. All this may, and doubtless does, proceed from modesty; but, permit me to tell you without any intention of wounding you, that it is a false modesty. It is right we, who are very dear to each other, should stand upon cold terms of courtesy and polite remarks. It would be inexpressible happiness for me to pour out my heart and love to you, if you too would act as kindly. I beseech you, my darling, to overcome your diffidence, and to treat me with frankness and affection.

I am in very good health, and enjoying as good spirits as usual.

If I possibly can I will come to see you next June. I look forward to the time of again meeting you with hope and anxiety. Remind Miss Lizzie that she owes me a letter.

Don't be angry, dear Lucy, at what I have said.

Your lover,
W. B. Butler

Fernandina. March 21, 1861

Dearest Lucy,

I, who have so often, perhaps unjustly, accused you of neglect, now plead guilty of the same offence. And yet I have an excuse, and a very good one too: I have been away from F—— for two weeks, engaged in such a way that it was impossible for me to write.

I have been dancing attendance at the sittings of the high and mighty "Circuit Court for the State of Florida," waiting for an opportunity, during a great press of business, to be examined for admission to the profession of law. Finally my petition was taken into consideration, and the examination granted me. I was so fortunate as to have on my committee three lawyers whose legal attainments were scarcely greater than my own, and the consequence was that I stepped into my "gown and wig" with perfect ease. I am now a lawyer by profession, and I trust may soon be one by practice also.

I am much grieved, dear Lucy, that any hasty words of mine should have caused you pain; and your gentle reproach has cut me to the heart. I am deeply ashamed that I have spoken so rudely and ungenerously to my dearest Lucy; and I pray that she will try to forget it, when I tell her that it was not through want of love but from excess of it.

It was very kind and good in you to write such an affectionate letter, and I am very grateful to you for it.

I fear that I cannot come to Virginia next June, yet I hope to be with you early in the fall.

Yours with much love,
Waddy Butler

Please excuse this unsatisfactory letter: I was on the sea today and am still half sea-sick.

Charlottesville. March 27, 1861

Dear Waddy,

Your long expected letter arrived yesterday; and much to my surprise I found you were still alive, and enjoying good health and spirits, and that you had been detained from writing only by being so fortunate as to have other business of more importance and interest. You cannot know how much relieved I felt at learning this.

Allow me to congratulate you on your having been admitted to the Bar; and I am quite surprised that you should have admitted a doubt of your passing the examination with ease, even had the lawyers been the best in the Southern Confederacy.

I am very sorry that you imagine that you have offended me for indeed it is a mistake, for I merely thought I would let you know that your accusation was unjust.

Charlie is becoming quite energetic, but I think he is inspired by his horse with which he seems to be quite enamoured. I believe that the chief virtue of the animal is to run away at the wrong time, for when he is particularly interested in conversation with a lady, the horse is sure to run off and leave the lady several miles behind.

The Students are making great secession demonstrations, and erected twenty flags, but I believe Louis is the only one who sets public opinion at defiance and has raised our national banner.[18]

18. The nearby University of Virginia, and other southern schools with male students, tended to be bastions of secessionist fervor. Louis was Lucy Wood's brother (b. 1855). In the 1860 census his name appears as *Lewis*.

I heard from Maggie yesterday, and she does not expect to stay in Washington much longer, but if she has to leave that place she will come here and stay with me until she gets another home.

You asked me some time ago, something [. . .][19]

Charlottesville. April 16, 1861

Dear Waddy,

I had a most agreeable surprise today in receiving a letter from you. It was a greater happiness than I had expected for I much feared that communication had ceased between us and the South; and though I can scarcely hope that this will ever reach you, I am so anxious that you shall hear from me once more when I am more amiable than when I last wrote that I will make the attempt, though I doubt not that Lincoln will have carried his threat into execution, of closing the mails, before this will have time to reach you.

We are expecting a dispatch every moment stating that Virginia has left at last this inglorious, disgraceful Union.[20] Yesterday I leveled Louis's Union flag to the ground with my own hands, though it was right hard work; and last evening we went to a farewell party given to Mr. Singleton who left with some of his friends for South Carolina this morning; and as soon as possible they will be followed by every Southerner here. The excitement is intense and I believe that every young man in Virginia would offer his services to our Sister Southern States, if it were not thought that they would very soon be needed at home.

Lizzie received a letter from you a day or two since, and I am sorry to say that for a time I was very angry with you for having sayed something about me that I did not like, but I have forgotten and forgiven that now.

What a long and dreary time it may be before it will be possible for me to see or hear from you again, and what wonderous changes will be wrought in that time.

19. The rest of the letter is torn off.

20. The state convention voted in Richmond on April 17, 1861, for Virginia to secede from the Union (secession was contingent on a state referendum, which was passed on May 23, 1861).

Would that I might be with you to try and comfort you in your sorrow; and alleviate the suffering you will have to pass through.

But wherever we shall meet, whether in Heaven or on Earth, I pray that you may bear the victor's palm.

With many Good wishes for your happiness both here and here after,

I remain as ever truly yours

LW

Fernandina. April 25, 1861

Dearest Lucy,

I am uncertain whether this will ever reach you, for I have heard that all the mails north of South Carolina have been discontinued, yet I will write now and run the chance of any letter reaching you, because it is probable that I may not have the like opportunity for a long time.

Let me explain myself. On tomorrow I shall leave this place for the purpose of recruiting men, in order to raise a company to go to the wars. As soon as I shall have accomplished that by obtaining a sufficient number, the company will be mustered into active service, and ordered to the scene of hostilities—perhaps to Pensacola, perhaps to Washington.

If I am successful in getting a company, I shall be ordered away on the first of May; If I am not, why then I shall go at any rate and without an order, for I am determined upon this, that I will stay no longer cooped in this place, where there is neither danger to be encountered nor glory to be won.

You will therefore know why it is, and you will not assign an improper cause should I at any time fail to write as often and regularly as I have done formerly.

I had set my heart, dear Lucy, upon seeing you next fall; but I fear that other and more imperative duties will prevent me. No men can tell when the strife just in its inception shall end; and until it does end, unless my life shall have sooner terminated, I devote myself to the cause of my country. She shall be my sole mistress, and at her feet am I content to cast everything.

If it so happens that I do not get a company, I will go wherever I list, and that will be where there is most likelihood of a fight. Should I come to Virginia, and it is probable that I may, I will ask you to marry me at once; though I can not take you to a home of my own before the war is over, and must leave you at your father's house until there is peace again. You will doubtless object to marrying a husband whom you will not perhaps see for years again, or at most only at long intervals; but I trust, dear Lucy, that my wishes, and, when I meet you, the arguments that I shall advance may overcome any scruples you entertain, no matter how strenuous they may be.

I thank heaven that Virginia has redeemed her tarnished honor, and you are no longer a foreigner to me.

Goodbye my darling. May God bless and protect you, my dearest love.

Yours,
Waddy Butler

Charlottesville. May 2, 1861

I was most charmingly surprised today, My Dear Waddy, by having a letter from you given me, for I had lost all hope of hearing from you for a long while, as I expected that you had already gone to Pensacola.

I think it strange that you did not receive my last letter, for although I feared much that it would never reach you, yet I should think that you might have gotten that, as yours has come to me.

The day after I last wrote to you the military companies of Charlottesville and the University were ordered off, and Oh! It was terrible, for we knew not where they were going, and we went to the depot to bid them farewell, and they left at twelve o'clock at night; and after we heard that they had gone to Harper's Ferry we heard false reports of the danger they were in, and that they were starving, so we busied ourselves sending provision, but they all returned in a week in good order, and joyful was our welcome home to them, but I would not have had one to have remained at home, nor would I now, and I labor hard all day making uniforms for the soldiers.[21] Among other things I make pantaloons,

21. In April 1861 the Charlottesville and University Battalion was formed. In May 1861 the Nineteenth Virginia Regiment was formed; it was composed of many Charlottesville area men.

and I expect to see for a good many days yet, certainly until the last man is equipped.

I hope you will decide on coming to Virginia; I cannot bare the thought of your being so far away, where I cannot know what has become of you, and we certainly need all of the assistance we can get. I am growing impatient for some action on our side. I cannot see that we are doing anything but allowing every advantage to be taken of us, but it is sayed that we are as yet entirely unprepared for a contest.

I have but little hope that this will ever reach you, and I trust that if it does not, you will pass it on your way to Virginia, where you will be welcomed by the state in general and by me in particular.

It is nearly if not quite Sunday morning, so I must say good night with many wishes for your health and happiness, and hoping that you will resist temptation and not allow feelings of hatred and revenge to take possession of you, but "trust God and fear not" and I know that you will be brave and noble.

Hoping to soon meet you I say Goodbye.

L.W.

Diary of
LUCY WOOD BUTLER
(April 17, 1861–July 3, 1863)

Charlottesville. April 17, 1861

The excitement is intense. Last week we heard rumors that a fleet had gone South, its destiny unknown, but it was supposed that it had gone to reinforce the forts.

Saturday evening I was hailed by Mr. Gordon of the cavalry corps and told that whilst he was drilling it had been announced that Fort Sumter had been taken by the South Carolinians and they had sent up a shout of exaltation and soon we heard that it had been done without loss of life and only two wounded.[1]

On Monday evening we went to Mrs. Peyton's to a little party given Richard Singleton who was summoned to S. Carolina to become Lieutenant in the army. I did not dance so I had a full benefit of the excited young men and whilst there we heard that Fort Perkins had been attacked, and today I heard $10,000 had been offered to the first who sealed the walls.[2]

1. The Confederacy won the Battle of Fort Sumter; the Union surrendered on April 13, 1861. There were no fatalities from the actual battle, but two Union men were killed in the ceremonial gun salute from an ammunitions explosion after the surrender. On April 15 President Lincoln called for seventy-five thousand volunteers to suppress the rebellion.

2. Wood is most likely referring to Fort Pickens. Fort Pickens was occupied by Union forces from January 10, 1861, the day of Florida's secession from the Union.

My Dear Maggie came from Washington with her family this morning. She is here with me, and when she left the City it had not been placed under martial law, but we have heard this evening that every public building and avenue had been guarded.

I was interrupted here to go to the depot to bid Charlie farewell, for the two foot companies of Charlottesville and two from the University were ordered off today to what place is not known though it is supposed that they are bound for Harper's Ferry, and, if such is the case, it is not thought that there will be any bloodshed, as it is now in the possession of a very few men, and they Virginians, but whatever is the result it is certainly very sad and brings home to us all that war has actually commenced. It will be awful when Washington is attacked which it will be in the course of a week. There were a great many ladies at the depot but they all seemed to imagine it was a festive occasion and their spirits were not at all depressed. I only saw Mr. Anderson and Charlie. They left at 10 o'clock this evening.

We heard today that Virginia had seceded but wished it to be private.[3]

April 18, 1861

We heard yesterday, and the news has been confirmed today, that Harper's Ferry was in the possession of our troops with the arms and machines of that place. Lincoln has been prevented from making an attack on them by not having sufficient force, but expected soon to be reinforced. We have just heard the glorious news that the 7th regiment of New York was turned back at Baltimore and the railroad torn up, so Monsieur the President has been disappointed.

Virginia has been declared out of the Northern into the Southern Confederacy.

This evening a secession flag was erected on the Rotunda, and speeches made by several of the Professors and others. A few weeks since one had been raised by the Students but they were requested to

3. See nn. 17 and 20 in "Letters" for information on Virginia's secession.

take it down. Now the banner of the Southern Confederacy waves triumphant with its eight bright stars amidst the approving shouts of all.[4]

I have not heard today anything of the forces from South Carolina.

Charlottesville. May 2, 1861

I am very cold and tired, for I have been busy all day making clothes for the soldiers at the Town Hall where all of the ladies assembled with their sewing machines today and yesterday, and we have worked right hard.

I have nearly completed a pair of pantaloons that I commenced yesterday.

I heard some sad news today, that poor Mr. Campbell Carrington had been accidentally shot in the thigh but I am glad to hear that the wound is not dangerous. Mrs. Carrington and James started for St. Louis this morning to see him.

I have not written for so long a time that I find in these exciting times the state of affairs quite different from what it was when I last wrote.

The military companies retuned exactly a week after their departure without having had any use for the lint and bandages I helped to prepare as the only enemy consisted in sobbing women whom they encountered in their search for the stolen arms that had been taken before their arrival. During a greater part of their journey they were greeted by shouts and music and the encouraging smiles and words of the ladies, but after passing Winchester all seemed like an enemy's country, for not one approving look or word did they receive. The last 18 miles they had to go on foot. When they arrived at Harper's Ferry they found that the Federal troops had just set fire to the place and run off.[5]

But only 2 buildings were burned and those of no great importance

4. The Rotunda is a building on the campus of the University of Virginia.

5. Harpers Ferry was a federal arsenal. It was the site of John Brown's raid in October 1859. In April 1861, Lieutenant Roger Jones set the Harpers Ferry arsenal on fire to prevent the Confederate forces from acquiring the Union weaponry.

as the flames had been extinguished and many of the arms rescued by the people. They found a great many arms had been secretly removed by orders from the government, but there were still 5,000 muskets and much very valuable machinery, a great deal of which was removed to Richmond, though some was left, and the manufacture still carried on, and several thousand men left to keep the place. They were under very poor command, and it is sayed that 100 regular troops could have cut them to pieces.

There was one of the most wonderfully stupid commands given ever heard of. There were several thousand northern men expected on the cars, and a company of sixty students were ordered to cross a covered bridge to the opposite side of the river. The bridge was ordered immediately to be blown up (there would have been no chance to recross but by swimming the river). They were to examine seventeen trains of cars and if one gun was fired it was to be a signal for the canon on the Virginia side to open on them, so if a gun had been accidentally fired their destruction would have been sure by the hands of their own men. They would have been soon cut to pieces if they had met so superior an enemy with all chance of escape cut off. But Providence was watching over them. The order for blowing up the bridge, though repeated several times and though the march was once burning, the order was disobeyed, no accident did occur, and the northern troops had left the train some fifteen miles below the place.

We had a meeting of the ladies over which Mrs. Carrington was requested to preside which she did in a most dignified and solemn way. She commenced by reading a suitable chapter and then prayed. She then told us that she had seen a letter from one of our men at Harper's Ferry stating that they were in great need of food, and advised us first to provide their comfort, so we soon dispersed to prepare provision, and five large boxes were sent off the next morning.

I went to work with great spirit but my ardour was cooled by persons telling me that they would never reach them. However I persisted and assisted in making the bread and sat up late fixing the things. I was amply repaid for the troops met the boxes as they were coming home and, but for them, they would have gone without either breakfast or dinner.

Every one was much excited on Wednesday from the morning till evening, as we would hear the troops were coming in an hour, and train after train arrived and we were disappointed, but when they came late in the afternoon feeling was most too deep for expression.

May 7, 1861

We have been busy sewing ever since last Thursday; "from morn to noon, from noon to dewy eve, the live long day," we sew, with the exception of Sunday, of course.[6]

The troops are pouring into Washington in great numbers, and now we are waiting for, instead of making, the attack.

Poor Maryland had been obliged to submit, and Lincoln had laid claims to Alexandria.[7] We (I am ashamed to say) are going to give the place up, for he has possession of the Potomac, and it would be impossible to keep it, though it should not go if I could help it without a struggle.[8] But it is now sayed that it is our policy to allow Lincoln to commence a triumphant march to Richmond, to surround him, and cut off all hope.

Troops are coming in from the South daily, and nearly a thousand men made their escape from Kentucky, and came on a few days since, in miserable condition, armed with stones.[9]

This place will in a day or two be the encampment of 2,000 men from several adjoining counties.

Charlie and John Magruder went to Lexington yesterday where they will remain and take a two months' course in military tactics. James Gilmer, Mr. Carrington, and several others speak of going on Thursday for the same purpose.

We heard that Mr. Campbell Carrington has been shot and was

6. John Milton's *Paradise Lost* (1667).

7. The Maryland Legislature voted 53–13 against secession on April 29, 1861.

8. Alexandria was occupied by the Union from May 24, 1861.

9. Kentucky governor Beriah Magoffin officially proclaimed Kentucky's neutrality at the beginning of the war.

wounded in the thigh. His mother started to see him immediately but heard before she had proceeded far on her journey (I was most happy to know) that he would soon be well, and would perhaps come on here, so she returned home, and is now very busy making cloathes to send him by the Gambles who start for St. Louis on Saturday. So I intend to sew for him tomorrow, he being a wounded Soldier and a friend.

May 9, 1861

The Riflemen and Monticello Guards went off to Culpepper to guard the railroad this morning.[10] I went on the street and told them goodbye as they marched past. Though I had not a friend and scarcely an acquaintance among them, yet the tears would come to my eyes, and I felt very sad, and every one looked so.

I spent the day at Mrs. Carrington's sewing for poor Campbell, and this afternoon I went to a Methodist prayer meeting, and was afterwards introduced to the minister, Mr. Early, also Mr. Annen.

Charlottesville. May 24, 1861

Sadder news reaches our ears every day. We have for some time expected to hear that Alexandria would be attacked. The cars arrived this afternoon, and it was announced that Lincoln had taken possession this morning without resistance.

Aunt Lizzie Harmon and family are the only relations who have yet left the place. They came last week and are now at Uncle Tom's and they think of boarding there.

The cavalry troop left a few days after our infantry, and they have all been stationed at Culpepper. We have heard from them quite often.

Ensign R. Lewis has written to Maggie quite often. He called with Mason Gordon and Willie Holbcome about six o'clock in the morning to tell us goodbye. He had a fine horse, and, as he started, Lydia handed him his beautiful banner.[11] He seized it in one hand and waved it aloft

10. The Monticello Guard (Company A) and the Albemarle Rifles (Company B) of the 19th Virginia Infantry Regiment.

11. Lydia was Wood's younger sister (b. 1843).

whilst he managed his "red roan steed" with the other. Oh! he did look splendid, he is so tall and dark. When I last heard from him, he was seated on the side of a hill, with his most ridiculous apron on that Maggie made and sent him, writing on the ground.

Poor fellows, they have many hardships to undergo, but we hear very cheering news from them: that there is but very little dissipation, and, what is far better than we could expect, their hearts seem to be turned unto God, and morning and evening they meet together to pray and give praise to His name.

I have spent all of my time sewing for the soldiers for the last three weeks, with the exception of the last two days when I was obliged to do some work for myself, and I now find myself completely broken down for I have taken no exercise except sometimes to walk up to a prayer meeting in the afternoon where we meet together to offer up prayers on behalf of our country, and those who have left this place for our defense.

Several companies have been stationed here, and have been supplied with comforts and necessities by our ladies, though we have not yet entirely equipped our own men yet, and there are two companies now here for whom we are working.

But what if we do grow weary, must we therefore stop? No, our needles are now our weapons, and we have a part to perform as well as the rest: we must make our men comfortable, we must encourage them by brave words and keeping stout hearts, we must try to turn their hearts to the guider of all destinies, and we must cry mightily unto Him day and night, and must trust in Him to deliver us. Yes, yes, we women have mighty work to perform for which we will be responsible. We have no glory, no fame to gain on earth, but it is ours to calm the fierce feelings of hatred and revenge, to be with and minister to the dying and the wounded; ours to point and lead the way for others—to attain for ourselves a glorious eternity and victory over our worst enemy.

May 27, 1861

This morning I went to the Depot to bid Mildred Watkins goodbye, and heard there had been an encounter at York Town in which seven hundred of the Federal troops had been killed and Butler taken prisoner. 90 of our men were said to be killed. This evening it was said to have taken place at Hampton, and some people believe it all to be a fable.[12]

I heard this afternoon that the Federal troops were advancing into Virginia, and that the scouts were in sight of each other, so the men who have left our little town will soon, I fear, have fighting enough at Manassas Gap, poor fellows.

I went to the Hall about ten this morning and made two cap covers for the Amherst Guardsmen stationed here and a portion of a jacket for the Montgomery Guards, or (as I call them) Ragged Rangers, the Company of which Mr. Bennet Taylor is Captain.

I left my work at sundown and started to walk alone, but met Mr. Crawford, one of the Amherst G——, who walked with me, and I enjoyed it very much, although he was telling of the hardships he and his fellow soldiers were undergoing, eating sea biscuits, etc.

After tea Dr. Lewis Randolph called and I had the pleasure of entertaining him alone. It was a great pleasure as he is as charming to me as he was that most happy spring, and we had one of our nice old talks of favorite books, just as we used to have in the days that are no more.

He is going to Lexington tomorrow and called to take a package to Charlie as he promised to do so several days ago when he called his Sister, Mrs. Hubbard. It was his first visit for two years.

Locust Hill. June 3, 1861

On Thursday, much to our surprise, Aunts Susan and Harriet and Grandmother arrived from Alexandria. It was with much difficulty that they obtained passports as Uncle Bob refused to take the oath. Old Mr. Caywood finally secured one as he was too old for service. They let him go but no men are now allowed to leave the place.

12. Union major general Benjamin Butler was assigned control of Fort Monroe in May 1861. It was during his time at Fort Monroe that Butler issued his infamous contraband policy: the refusal to return fugitive slaves to their owners.

They finally left by private conveyance. As soon as they came in sight of our sentinels, they were besieged with questions: "What is the news, etc.?" When they arrived at Manassas Junction they were treated with the greatest courtesy and shown every attention by the troops. The officers gave them their chamber and parlor to occupy that night. They met many of their friends who had escaped from Alexandria. The next day they came to Charlottesville on the cars.

There is much discussion about Jackson of Alexandria who met Capt. Elsworth (the morning the place was invaded) on the stair with his flag of the Confederacy which Jackson had sworn should wave on his house or else he would die in its defense. His seeing the Capt. was the first intimation he had of the invasion and he fired on him which proved fatal and the fire was returned by the Federal soldiers present. Both died instantly and Jackson's body was guarded for some hours and no one allowed to see it. Some say he was not a brave man, only a desperate one. Others make a hero of him. I think with the latter class. His brother vowed vengeance, and many ridiculous stories are told of him, though it is sayed to be really true that he has killed eight of the Federal pickets.[13]

I preserve some verses on this subject, not because of any merit in the piece but merely as a memento of the deed, for I am glad that there was at least one man who would not yield to his country's dishonor without a struggle.

On Friday night we had a skirmish at Fairfax Court House but I do not know any of the particulars.[14]

Lizzie thinks of going to Lexington Wednesday with Millie Cochran

13. Colonel Elmer Ellsworth, who was a friend of Abraham Lincoln, was shot and killed by James Jackson when Ellsworth tried to remove the Confederate flag from Jackson's Marshall House Inn. He was the first Union officer killed in action. In retaliation Corporal Francis Brownwell killed Jackson.

14. On June 1, 1861, a Union cavalry raid occurred at Fairfax County Courthouse. Captain John Quincy Marr was killed; he became the first Confederate officer killed in action.

and the Carringtons and I have no doubt that she will have a delightful visit as Charlie, Lewis Randolph, and so many of our friends are now there. I thought of going too once as I was afraid I might never have another opportunity of enjoying the Grand and beautiful scenery, but as there was a little uncertainty about it, and as I do not think this is a time for gayety or pleasure trips, and as there were some other objections, I thought I would come up here as I had promised her and myself too some time since, especially as she is going to stay here now for we have so many people at home. I expect to enjoy Aunt Lucy and the quiet time very much.

Charlie Benson put us on the cars and gave Maggie a bouquet. I think his heart has been touched.

We also saw Mr. Slack and Mr. Early.

Locust Hill. June 7, 1861

Yesterday afternoon, although it was very muddy, yet it had stopped raining for awhile, and, as we had not been out for several days, Aunt Lucy and myself went to Uncle Lewis's and Maggie came home with us.

After tea we decided to go to a prayer meeting held weekly at different houses in Woodville. Last evening it met at Mr. Suttler's in an "upper chamber." It is the house that claims the honor of being my birthplace, though it has been so much changed that it can scarcely be recognized.

Mr. Snyder conducted the meeting and, when he requested any one who wished to make remarks to come forward, Mr. Dinwiddie arose and repeated St. Paul's words, "press forward to the mark set before you." He spoke with modest confidence and, as the words flowed from his eloquent lips, his eye kindled and his face looked as though it had been lightened by a ray from heaven. No one could have listened to his appeal to Christians without being greatly benefitted or to the unredeemed without being much affected. He then prayed a beautiful prayer.

I was sorry for it but Maggie laughed and talked a great deal on our way home which I saw grated so on his feelings and she regrets it now. Cousin Matilda laughed at me yesterday for saying that he was the most perfect man, or rather near perfection, in every respect than any I have ever met. He has never been society and rather avoids it, yet his manner is easy and ever that of a dignified gentleman. It is true he lacks a little polish and knows little of fashionable etiquette, yet his true refinement of mind and soul are such that he never does a rude or unrefined thing, and then, by his superior mind and elevated Christian character, he seems never by one word to forget that Christ has come into the world to save us.

We hear every day of the most atrocious acts that our northern friends (who are so earnestly striving for a reunion with their sister states) are committing, and that in Western Virginia where the population is nearly composed entirely of abolitionists they are advancing rapidly upon us, and are now within 150 miles of Staunton, 3000 in number.[15] One hundred of our men lay in ambush, fired upon them, and killed 90 of their number, and five of our own men were found dead, but this put no stop to their march, and we are being surrounded on all sides. This news we heard this morning, and yesterday we heard there had been a contest at Philippi between two small bodies of men and our forces to retreat.[16]

I have read a full account of the attempt at taking Fairfax Court House. Last Saturday morning early a large company of cavalry rode through the place shouting several times and firing pistols in every direction. Capt. Marr was rushed forward, was shot, his men who were camped at one end of town became confused, but some one took the command, rallied them, marched on the enemy, killed 17 of them, took some very fine horses, arms, etc., and the enemy left in haste. Capt Marr was our only loss but that was one much regretted, and he was a brave, high minded man.[17]

15. Western Virginia, a stronghold of Unionist support, seceded from the state of Virginia and joined the Union on June 20, 1863, as the state of West Virginia.

16. The Union forces won the Battle of Philippi in Barbour County, Virginia (now West Virginia), on June 3, 1861. This was a minor land battle in the war and took place before the Battle of First Manassas (Bull Run) on July 21, 1861.

17. Contrast Wood's account of events at Fairfax County Courthouse with that given in n. 14 in "Diary."

Locust Hill. June 8, 1861

This morning a train took a body of men and some cannons to protect Western Virginia from the Ohio invaders, and we hear Lexington is in great danger.

I heard from home today. Lydia wrote a short note saying that Lizzie and her party had not gone yet, though think of starting to Lexington on Wednesday next. Mr. Carrington has arrived but expects to leave next week so I fear I shall not see him.

Much to my surprise, Camp Goodloe was announced, and I was happy to welcome him as one more gallant soldier from the South who has come to defend us. Oh! how changed he is since I first saw him. He then was fair and so interesting and I thought smart, though I was rather surprised at his entertaining me at Sallie Pride's wedding by reading kiss verses. He is much taller now, sunburnt and thin, with an effort at red whiskers, but I will still like him. He remained until late in the afternoon.

Warwick was here then for a few moments, then Mrs. and Dr. Woods, and Mr. Nealson. When the doctor left he tried to take that gentleman with him but the latter declined.

Mr. Overton got his pistols and I had two nice fires, struck my mark both times with a steady hand, much to the delight of Nealson whom I fear I teased too much, but, notwithstanding, he spent the evening and promised to call again.

After tea, Maggie and Mr. Woods, from Bloomfield, came in. Mr. Dinwiddie returned from Charlottesville so we had quite a gay party, but Uncle Merry has disappointed me very much by breaking up a colored Sunday school that Mr. Dinwiddie and I were trying to establish. I had thought of it for so long and was much interested in the cause.

Locust Hill. June 10, 1861

Sunday morning we went to Sunday school, Maggie with us, and she, having made the arrangement the evening before, took a class of boys with Mr. Nealson and Mr. Overton, over which she presided with great dignity. Aunt Lucy gave me half of her class which I took great pleasure in teaching.

The school over, we went to church at St. Paul's, the first time I have been there since it has been enlarged and very much improved. Willie Meade read the service and a sermon, Mr. Nealson being absent.

I fear I did not spend the day very well for I was with Mr. Dinwiddie and Mr. Overton nearly all of the afternoon, and then Camp Goodloe came, and presently proposed a walk over to see Maggie in which Mr. Dinwiddie joined us.

Maggie was very much excited as her uncle, Dr. John Wood, from Louisiana, had just spent the day there and insisted on her going home with him, with the promise of calling for her in ten days and stopping anywhere she likes, and when she gets to his home of having horse and carriage at her disposal and command. Although they are Roman Catholics, she is of course delighted, especially as Victor is there, and they all speak French, and I do not think it will grieve her much to leave us all.

This morning Uncle Merry's nephew, D. Anderson, arrived from western Virginia with very sad news of the enemy's rapid approach and many depredations.

I went for the first time I have been since I came here to pay my usual visit to the graveyard quite alone this afternoon. It was in better condition than I expected to find it, and was so peaceful and quiet that I could not bear to leave, but I had promised to go to see Maggie so I had to go. She came home with me and stayed until after tea.

I finished reading *Nicholas Nickleby* today which I commenced on Tuesday—very much pleased, of course.

Spring Hill (Virginia). June 12, 1861

Yesterday morning I took Walter to the cars and sent him home.[18] Mollie and I then walked to Aunt Maria's and remained until this morning, when we walked here.

I have been quite busy today and yesterday making an underbody for Maggie, and many times did I have to pull the work out, and I have not quite finished it yet.

This afternoon two gentlemen called for me, and, when I went

18. Walter was her younger brother (b. 1849).

down, I found Mrs. Nealson and Woods. They had started to Locust Hill but heard that I was not there so they met Mr. Dinwiddie, and went with him to Aunt Maria's where he, not finding me, returned home, but the others were more persevering and came here, and were rewarded for their trouble by beholding me with a beautiful red nose. They stayed until quite late.

How changed everything is here from what it was when I last had visitors here.

Rose Hill (Virginia). June 15, 1861

Thursday was a day of solemn fasting and prayer for our dear country and our own preservation and it was strictly observed.[19]

This evening we heard that the enemy are at Earlysville where they have killed three families within fifteen miles of us. We are not frightened although nearly all of the men have left us, what few were left, for the scene of action. We are not frightened for we trust God and fear no evil.

This report may be false but we have reason to believe it true. Our men, brave as they are, may be repulsed, may be overpowered, but we will pray God that it may not be so, and we will trust His arm rather than an arm of flesh. And He will surely be with us if we cry aright, will give us strength to bear up under our afflictions, and, even if He should think it best that our lives would be taken away, He will, if we pray fervently and trust Him, take care of our souls.

The report has been confirmed. Henry and Uncle Lewis have left, giving orders for the servants to arm themselves.

I trusted and prayed to Him and found that no men had lifted up his hand against us, and my anxiety (for I had no fear) was turned into thanksgiving. I was hastening over to be with Aunt Lucy who had sent all of her boys off, Merry and Mr. Overton, no one else of any size being at home, when I met nearly at the house a buggy, out of which a Gentleman stept, one I have been watching and waiting for some time. He assured

19. Jefferson Davis declared nine official days of fasting throughout the Civil War; see nn. 41, 52, and 75 in "Diary."

me that it was all a false report, and I immediately sent Maggie word, and that she and Miss Carrie Morrill should come over, which they did.

I then found it too late to think of going to C—— that evening as it was proposed and postponed until the evening.

I felt very sad at parting with Maggie and fear we shall never meet again, but I shall try and come to see her before she starts to Louisiana. It is quite uncertain her going now as a large force is marching against Winchester, and her uncle will be sure to be engaged in the battle.

Merry returned from the scene of action very weary and hungry and sayed the whole report had been sent abroad on account of a horrible murder that took place last night. 3 negro men broke into an overseer's house, and murdered his wife. One of the negroes was shot by the man, the other two fled, and have not yet been taken.[20] There were a thousand men assembled today and reports and telegrams sent to Richmond and other places stating that the Federal troops were upon us, but this will do some good. It will keep off trouble by showing how soon and in what numbers we can rally.

> "I go but whereso'er I flee,
> There's not an eye will weep for me;
> There's not a kind congenial heart
> Where I can claim the meanest part."[21]

So says Mr. Dinwiddie. I cannot agree with him. I am sorry he is away and I cannot say Goodbye.

Charlottesville. June 24, 1861

I have been anxious to record the events of the past week as they transpired, not that anything strange or wonderful has occurred, but

20. I was unable to find any evidence of these murders. This is not to suggest that Charlottesville did not struggle with race and violence. In one notorious instance, in early 1863 four slaves killed an officer attempting to impress them into Confederate service.

21. Lord Byron's "Stanzas to a Lady, on Leaving England" (1809).

they may be connected intimately with my thoughts of the past all through life. I have been prevented by want of time, and the weather, until today, has been so warm that I have been exhausted.

Sunday morning early I came with Mr. Butler in a buggy (that detested vehicle) to Charlottesville in time to go to church and hear Mr. Slack preach one of his erratic sermons.

That evening Mr. McCarley and Mr. Major called to take the ladies to church. Lydia went with the former gentleman, but I had an engagement with Mr. Butler, in consequence of which Mr. Major accompanied himself and his white kid gloves.

Cousin Lucy Maury asked me to bring Mr. Butler to her house and as he consented, and asked me to ride to Farmington with him, we concluded to spend the day and evening in the country.

I discovered early on Tuesday morning that Lizzie had left no riding habit behind her, so, after due consideration, I concluded to borrow from Kate Stockton who immediately went to work with great spirit helping to alter her dress so as to make it fit me. Finally I was all equipped for the ride, three hours after the time appointed.

Mr. Butler rode Charlie's Pegasus who succeeded in blistering the rider's hands as he was gloveless, but we spent such a pleasant day that all trials were soon forgotten. Mr. Butler especially seemed to enjoy it as we had plenty of fruit and I think he has rather a weakness for such things.

We started for Mr. Maury's just as the sun was setting, and after a charming ride we arrived to find every one expecting us with some anxiety as they were afraid that Charlie's horse might have proved dangerous.

I changed my habit for a light evening dress and passed the evening quite agreeably. Although Ms. Boston was there much to Betty's annoyance, Mr. Summerfield Smith was with us who is very smart and entertaining, and Mr. Nase, a nice little Presbyterian preacher.

Cousin Lucy insisted on our not leaving until the next morning, and being fatigued we consented but left early next morning on plea of business, for Mr. Butler expected to leave next morning in search of Gen. Burnham of whom he wished to ask a commission.

My labors of the day consisted in making a tobacco bag and talking.

Cousin John Dean came in the afternoon and sayed that he would take Maggie away next morning. I was very very sorry that she should have to go without my talking to her once more, but I had to content myself with going to the depot and seeing her whilst the cars stopped. Her mother was going as far as Richmond with her, and I was surprised to see Maggie in such fine spirits as she will probably not return for several years, but she seemed so much excited and delighted that she had nearly forgotten the consideration of leaving her friends. I know that she had said something harsh and unkind to Robert Lewis, and had not since had an opportunity of writing to him, so I carried paper and a pencil, and gave her a note saying what she would do with it, for, as Mr. Butler was going as far as Gordonsville (on his way to Manassas Junction) with her, I thought she could write a reconciling note to Robert and send it by him.

Cousin Lucy told Mr. Butler that we would make his cloathes for him, so, after many notes to and from Mr. Brockman, she and I went on Main Street Thursday evening, the day on which Maggie left, and purchased four calico shirts, and she took me home with her to help make these into two fatigue jackets and other minor affairs.

We sent for Aunt Susan the next morning and she, Betty, Cousin Lucy, and myself, went to work with the assistance of sewing machines, but were interrupted early in the afternoon by the advance guard of five cavalry companies, and we did very little sewing the rest of the day.

Cousin Lucy sent the first party of soldiers everything she could find to eat or drink in the house, and the poor fellows seemed to need it. They seemed so very much fatigued and they were so dusty it would have been impossible to have recognized an acquaintance among them.

Some of the men seemed so much in need of havelocks, for very few were provided with them, that we made a dozen or more, after a pattern that I invented, for the next who passed, whilst Cousin Lucy had a barrel of cider, large tubes of ice water, punch, and sangaree, carried to the fence, with every description of drinking vessel, from the silver goblet to the tin cup, and all of us, with the exception of Aunt Susan and Miss Carrie, stood on the inside of the fence, and would help the cavaliers as they passed by, and very grateful they seemed, and many the kind wishes and promises they made of returning with a piece of Lincoln's scalp, though we told them we would rather they should return with their own unharmed.

The servants seemed quite as enthusiastic as their masters, and nearly all of the three hundred men rode off gaily, cheering us as they went.

We took tea that evening by moonlight, under the large oak tree.

The next day being Saturday and we, expecting Mr. Butler to return on that day and take his final departure for the army on the following Monday, sewed busily until late in the afternoon when we had accomplished our work with the exception of a pair of garters that Miss Carrie promised to finish and bring to church with her the next day if Mr. Butler would take care of a fair haired cousin of hers that he might meet in the Federal army. Cousin Lucy and I then came into town, and met Mr. Butler on the street who had returned the day before after an unsuccessful expedition.

I found that Charlie had returned from Lexington on Friday and was then in the country trying to get up a company, and I think he met with some success. He did not return until yesterday evening. He is looking well and seems to be in good spirits.

Lydia escorted me to the church last night and hastened me so that I forgot until I started to put on my shoes, and, when I found myself on the street with a pair of large heelless morning slippers on my feet, my sensations were by no means agreeable, but Mr. Nealson preached such a good sermon that I did not mind my slippers coming home, but Lydia was seriously incommoded by not securing another escort.

[Undated entry]

As many and as great as are the subjects of public interest, I shall first turn to a page in my own private life in which a leaf has been turned of as much importance to me as the wonderful affairs of state are to the rest of the world.

On Wednesday evening, 10 o'clock, July 3rd, 1861, I was united to W. B. Butler by Mr. Meade in the presence of a few near relatives and several friends.

I did not decide on taking this step until a few days before, and I did not altogether approve of it, but Mr. Butler urged it so much that

I thought it best to consent, so on Monday we thought it best to make some slight preparation consisting of one suit of cloathes in which a solid stone coloured silk played a conspicuous part, the dress which I was to wear that evening, but the morning before the ceremony was performed my friends sayed that they could not see me with the dress on, and that I must wear white.

So a plain muslin skirt wad made to a dress I had trimmed with handsome lace; a tulle veil, some cape jessamines that Goochey sent me were hastily arranged, my hair perfectly plain, and I found myself in white from finger to toe, and dressed as simply as possible, for I would not have worn anything handsome or expensive at such a time as this.

I recovered to some extent from the state of extreme agitation and low spirits (in which I had been for the two last days) before the ceremony commenced. After it was over and the congratulations were finished, I took a seat near Mr. Dinwiddie, the only Gentleman I had asked to be present, and he talked with me all the evening, not moving except once when we went to look at a comet whose trail, though not very wide or brilliant, extended across half the heavens.

I told Mr. Dinwiddie goodbye that evening as he left next morning with his company, the Students, for Lewisburgh, to join Wise's Brigade, and, as Mr. Butler had joined the same company, I told Mr. Dinwiddie of his having been baptised in the Episcopal church that afternoon, and as he had a so much longer religious experience (and I really think him the best Christian I ever saw) I asked him to speak with Mr. Butler on the subject. At last he overcame his bashfulness sufficiently to leave and say goodbye though it cost him great exertion.

The two Saunders, M. Woodson, and Kate, with Aunt Lucy, Uncle Merry and son, Cousin Lucy, Betty and Nannie, composed, with the immediate family, the entire company.

Kate, Texy, and Cousin Lucy and her girls, came that morning and were at work all day for me, and they each gave me a pretty present which were the only ones I received except some from Aunt Susan and Anne, and Grandma, and the handsomest one was given by Charlie, a silver card case.

It was decided that evening at ten o'clock that I should accompany

Mr. Butler who was going to Richmond next day to try and get a commission from Sec. Mallory and, though I was totally unprepared for anything of the kind, Cousin Lucy sayed I must go and that she would have my trunk ready in the morning, and so I found it, with everything needed in it for she had made up the deficiencies in my wardrobe by borrowing from Betty and everyone she could. She did everything to relieve me from trouble or embarrassment, and I scarcely think I could have gone through with it all but for her assistance, and all of my friends were as kind as they could be, and far more than I deserved.

We spent several days pleasantly at the Exchange where I saw many soldiers in every imaginable uniform, among the rest three new cousins in the Hampton Legion, one of them captain of a cavalry company in which Richard and Carter Singleton are privates.

We enjoyed the drive out to see this Legion drill very much, especially as Cousin Matilda was with us, and she remained all the evening, and Charlie and Jimmy Gilmer were with us that evening, the best we spent in the city.

I have not heard from Mr. Butler but once since he left, and that letter was written the day after he arrived in Lewisburgh, but he left that place the day he wrote, for Charleston, and I fear will not receive my answer in his letter.

I spent several days this week at Cousin Lucy's which very much improved my health.

Charlottesville. July 19, 1861

I am very weary though I will try and write a few lines.

We have all been in great excitement this week about the dreadful news from Western Virginia, and we have heard such shocking reports that it is not strange that some should have considered our State already a conquered province. After we received correct accounts it was bad enough, for Garnett has certainly been killed, and several hundred under Colonel Pegram cut to pieces; many, at least the company from Hampton Sydney, taken prisoners but sent home on parole, and the Regiment obliged to retreat, but we have sent so many men over since then and Gen. Lee is going to take command now that we apprehend no danger.[22]

We heard yesterday that Gillum's Regiment (in which Charlie and Jimmy Gilmer are employed as drill masters with pay and officers' privileges) would go up to Staunton that morning so to the depot we went, and, after working an hour or two, we had the pleasure of seeing an empty train nearly and no soldiers, after which we returned home.

Just after supper it was again sayed the cars were coming, and Texy, Lydia, and myself ran to the depot as fast as we could, I with my morning slippers on and my hair streaming in the wind, and just as we reached the hotel the cars started, but we kept on, and fortunately found Mr. D. Danis who told us that it was an empty train, and took us to the parlor.

After I had composed my straying locks and more scattered thoughts, but before we were seated, he called to us that the train was coming, and, as we went down the steps, Lydia was so much excited that she gave one loud shriek.

We found Mother and Father and several others awaiting us on the steps, but we expected the cars to leave in ten minutes, and there were a thousand men aboard, so we soon lost sight of them, ran away down the road, and, at length, got between trains where it was quite dark. Followed by Lydia and W. Meade, I ran down to the road inquiring for Witcher's Co. when I met Charlie and bore him triumphantly back to the rest of the party. He promised to stay all night with us and rejoin his Regiment today.

Whilst all of this excitement was going on we heard of the flight at Manassas, and soon it was confirmed, and the fact that we were *victo-*

22. The Battle of Rich Mountain (July 11, 1861) in Randolph County, Virginia (it would become West Virginia in 1863), resulted in a Union victory. The Union withstood approximately fifty casualties and the Confederacy three hundred. Confederate lieutenant colonel John Pegram surrendered on July 13; Brigadier General Robert Garnett was killed in a skirmish at Corrick's Ford on the same day.

rious, and it is sayed that we had only 25 killed, the enemy 1500, but I expect that this is an exaggerated account.[23]

I stood on the hotel steps for some time for Texy was there with Willie Fields for whom she had been looking and searching for some time, and I felt not at all afraid to talk with the soldiers, although I object so much to it generally.

I have been most of the day attending sick soldiers for there are 500, if not more, here, and I have ten under my charge, at least to some extent for my Mother and Aunt Mary attend the same, and tomorrow morning I will have to go early and take their breakfasts, and, as it is now very late, I must stop.

July 23, 1861

The news from Manassas that I mentioned in my last was to some extent correct: the battle took place at Bulls Run, the enemy was forced to retreat after fighting from five in the morning to the same hour in the evening, 60 of our men were killed, and 500 of the enemy.[24] It is sayed that the enemy did not bury their dead, for, when they were permitted to do so, they commenced throwing up breastworks. Patterson marched to reinforce the enemy, Johnson followed him to assist us.[25]

On Saturday morning I went to the hospital and remained until the afternoon. Aunt Anne and Aunt Mary were with me part of the time. I found a great deal to keep me busy besides the men under my special charge for there were many suffering for attention, and I went to the relief of as many as I could.

23. The Battle of First Manassas (First Bull Run) was fought on July 21, 1861. Brigadier General Irvin McDowell led the Union forces; Brigadier Generals Joseph Johnston and P.G.T. Beauregard led the Confederate forces. Approximately 28,500 Union forces and 32,000 Confederate forces were engaged in the battle. It is estimated that the Union endured approximately 3,000 casualties and the Confederacy 1,800. The battle resulted in a Confederate victory.

24. See n. 23 in "Diary."

25. She is most likely referring to Brigadier General Joseph E. Johnston.

In the room in which there were 6 S. Carolinians, one of the men was quite sick with measles, the rest convalescent. One seemed a very good religious young man and offered his bed to any who was worse than he was.

In the other room there were four Mississippians of the 18th Regiment, a Corporeal Ellison, a W. King, Gowin and Guise, and they were all nearly well, and seemed to enjoy good spirits. As the room was wanted for men that were much worse, Mother and I fixed Charlie's room, and sent for them yesterday morning where they seem to have been enjoying themselves ever since, playing on Charlie's violin, and smoking and reading, until they say it looks like home, but the books remind them of school. Still they were very impatient to go back to camp, and it was sayed yesterday that their captain had been killed in the engagement the day before.

Sunday, the 21st, the belligerent forces met at 5 in the morning and fought until eight in the evening. Three different points were attacked. Bulls Run was again the scene of action, the enemy retreated several times, and was finally routed. The Cavalry was in pursuit until eleven o'clock that night. Major Sherman was killed, and the coach and six of that arch traitor Scott were taken, but he also had escaped. Gen. Beauregard's horse was shot from under him. Jef. Davis arrived late in the action on the field, and the Hampton Legion came late in the day. No one knows how many were killed and wounded on either side, but altogether the killed and wounded have been estimated at 15,000 men, but the saddest occasion of the day was the consequence of a mistake.[26]

Our men had adopted a badge consisting of a strip of red flannel tied around the arm. The Yankees found us out, and a Regiment of their men adopted it, and with our flag marched right up to our men before they were detected but, when they were, our men charged bayonets, and put them to flight. Then two of our Regiments, it is yet

26. Another (exaggerated) account of the Battle of First Manassas. See n. 23 in "Diary."

uncertain which, marched up and were mistaken for Yankees trying the same deception again. They were fired into and cut down nearly to a man before the mistake was discovered.[27]

It rained in torrents all yesterday, and they were bringing the sick, wounded, and dying, up on the cars, and many were left exposed to the weather before places could be provided for them. I did not go out at all for Mother does not like me to stay at the hospital for a long time, and there would have been no use going for a little while, but Cousin Lucy Maury was out all day collecting linen and bandages for the wounded. She came here and changed her cloathing once as one suit was perfectly wet although she had a hack impressed into her service, for her carriage had gone home.

It is strange how composed we can all be under this, surrounded by the dead and the dying and the suffering soldiers, our own friends, even those nearest and dearest to us, far away and exposed to every danger, and even now, for what we know, may be lying cold on their faces with a bullet through their hearts, and the bright sun shining heedlessly on them, and cool fresh air blowing lightly on their hair, and we know not at what moment we may hear of a defeat at one of the "five points" we have to defend, any one of which, if lost, would bring ruin upon us. Half of this would have been enough to have turned us heart sick, and made us exclaim, "This is more than I can bear," if we had only thought of it a few months since, but it has come gradually upon us. Little by little did the cloud spread, blacken, and advance, and, now it has burst upon us, seems not so terrible as it did at first. Some are strong hearted, others cannot realize, and we all have so much to keep our hands, our heads, and our hearts busy that we have not time to mourn, and to those who trust in our God nothing will be too much for them, nothing can overpower.

27. Not only did the Union and (the first) Confederate flags look similar, but uniforms were often not standardized. As a result, both sides could fall victim to friendly fire. A new Confederate flag, less similar to the U.S. flag, was adopted in May 1863.

Farmington. August 6, 1861

I find that two weeks ago I attempted to give an account of the battle at Manassas, the greatest that has ever taken place on this continent, and I find that I made many mistakes as I had only heard flying reports, but since then I have seen several persons who were in the engagement of that day, one of them was Camp Goodloe who came on for a day or two with a sick friend, and he seemed so much affected that his eyes would fill with tears whenever he spoke of it.

Mr. Cooper, a Gentleman and noble soldier who is sick at our house, gave me more information than anyone else.

A hundred thousand men were engaged during the day, 80,000 of the enemy came against 20,000 of our men. We fought bravely, desperately, but we are obliged to retreat several times, and some of our regiments were thrown into confusion for awhile by mistaking their own men for the enemy, and firing upon them; they fought for some time in low pine thickets. In the middle of the day Johnson arrived with 15,000 fresh men, our fortunes changed immediately, both sides fought well, but at last the enemy fled. Their batteries had been stormed just in the face of their fire, and they left behind them all of their artillery, the boasted Sherman's battery said to be invincible and all, besides numbers of arms of all kinds, and it is sayed 8,000 of their men dead on the field, a number of wounded and prisoners. Many high officers fell. It is sayed that they rushed through Alexandria like mad men, without hats, without arms, or anything they could throw away.[28]

We found a large number of handcuffs, and some of the prisoners have confessed that they were so sure of victory that these irons had been brought to place on Southern Soldiers whom they could use as breastworks in case of resistance at Richmond.

Many Congressmen and Ladies had come in carriages from Wash-

28. Again, this is an exaggerated account of the Battle of First Manassas, particularly in terms of Union forces engaged (80,000) and Union deaths (8,000). See n. 23 in "Diary."

ington to witness our defeat, and had brought dresses, champagne, and, in short, made every preparation for a fiendlike ball that night, whilst their dearest friends, and, at any rate their countrymen might be dead or dying in the field before them, and thus they would celebrate the carnage. But God in his mercy would not permit His earth to be polluted by such an unholy act, and the same hour when they had thought to be moving lightly to music they were fleeing with "such haste as fear and cowardice can make" to the music of their panting breath and beating heart.

It is not known, and may never be, how great our loss is, but, this we know, that it was very heavy, and, it is sayed, nearly as much as that of the enemy.

Oh! It was a Glorious victory, but not one that we would celebrate with wild revelry, for none seems to rejoice. How could we when we think of the noble hearts that have ceased to beat and the sufferings of the wounded, for if our dear soldiers had been spared we could but have sorrowed at the sufferings of the foe, and not rejoiced, but many hearts have been lifted in gratitude to the throne of Him who preserved us, and have thanked Him for his protection and this wonderful deliverance. But for this our homes would now be desolate and Virginia would be no more.

I came to Farmington on Sunday a week ago to stay with Cousin Lou. Mother and Aunt Mary have been working very hard since then, and two of their patients have died, which of course distressed them very much. One of them was a Mr. Myers, the other, Mr. Hemphill. They were both from S. Carolina, had friends with them, and were very nice young men.

Aunt Mary and two of her convalescent boys, little Messrs. Massie and Garrison of S. Carolina, spent Wednesday with us, and Friday Cousin Lou and I went to town and stayed all day.

We met Mr. Cooper who rode out with us in the morning. Father was told of his being ill at the Central Hotel, and took him to our house the day after I left home. He was there very ill, just recovering from the effects of a haemorrhage of lungs, and he had the pneumonia, but when we saw him he was well enough to walk downstairs, and very tall and thin he looked, and had it not been for his inimitable expression, especially when he smiled, he would not have been handsome. I think he is something like Charlie Conrad, though much older, I suppose he is thirty or more. He is a widower with four children and says he is engaged to Cornelia—I know not what. He is a Gentleman Farmer from Mississippi, Madison County Canton, and Judge of the County Court, and I suppose a politician, and one of the leading men of his country.

He expresses the most noble sentiments and seems one of the most highminded, honourable men I have ever met with, and he is certainly very charming and agreeable, and has love for all flowers, especially cape jessamine, so on my way out here that evening I stopped at Mrs. McKennie's, and she was so kind as to give me the only cape jessamine she had.

We stopped by for Mr. Strange who requested us to do so. He is quite a handsome agreeable young Gentleman but he has not yet joined the army and I, of course, cannot like him much.

We found Miss Mattie Duke and M. Roades here, and they have not gone home yet.

The next morning we sent the carriage in town which returned with Lizzie, Aunt Susan, Mr. Cooper and a servant.

I thought the musical box would burst all bounds as all day long it played, and yet, when eveningtide was ended, its sweet notes still ascended, and, what was yet more charming, figs, plums, and Gooseberrys were universally admired, and, altogether, we had quite a pleasant day and evening.

The next day was Sunday and most of the party dispersed. Among the rest Mr. Cooper went in. He took the cape jessamine and some other flowers home with him, and sayed he intended to send them to Cornelia. He went to church but looked so weak and badly that I went home with him before the services were over. Mr. Cooper sayed he expected to return to the army on Wednesday in spite of my, and all of our, earnest solicitude that he should not do so, but would go home into the South. But he is so much afraid that his honor will be compromised, and so anxious to be with his brother who is a private solider that he will sacrifice his life, for he even feels that he will surely die if he goes to the army in a very short time.

I wished to remain at home Sunday but Miss Roades could not return by herself, so I got Mr. Ellison and Gowin and brought them out with me.

I sent Mr. Cooper some flowers and tomatoes yesterday, and he sent a very pleasant note in return to Cousin Lou and myself.

I received a letter from Mr. Butler today, the second one I have had since I have been here. He says he is quite well with the exception of a cold which I fear is not slight. He has retreated with Wise's army to Lewisburgh.

Charlottesville. August 15, 1861

Mr. Butler left me this morning, after having paid a visit for a week. He came the day after my return from Farmington (which was last Wednesday).

Lieut. Dinwiddie called the day before his arrival, told me that they were then encamped at White Sulphur Springs where they expected to remain several weeks, but Mr. Sparrow came over yesterday and told me this evening that Wise had advanced fifteen miles toward Gauley again, and, as he has been reinforced by Floyd's joining him, and it is sayed that Gen. Lee will take large reinforcements over and take the command, it is supposed they will make an attack on Gauley very soon.

Mr. Butler took me to Farmington Monday afternoon, and we went from thence the next morning to Locust Hill, and Cousin Matilda and all from Uncle Lewis's came over to see us.

Aunt Lucy had two sick soldiers with her, one of them our old acquaintance of Bloomfield, Mr. Burley Jones; the other his friend.

We went to Mr. Maury's in the afternoon and came home for tea.

After many difficulties, Mr. Butler succeeded in getting a servant, just as he was starting off, and most fortunate it was, for, heretofore, he has been obliged to cook for the mess and wash his cloathes, services not calculated to please a gentleman or a soldier by any means.

We fixed Mr. Butler a box to which Aunt Lucy and Aunt Mary contributed, but I am afraid that, as his company have moved, he will have to leave it.

Mr. Ellison and Gowin and Mr. Garrison have all left and we have no one now but a Mr. Harper, an innocent good plain boy from Georgia, and Mr. Cooper is still here though he expects to leave in a day or two.

Charlottesville. August 28, 1861

I spent most of last week at Mr. Maury's and at the Delevan military hospital assisting Cousin Lucy who had a dozen soldiers to nurse, most of them fever cases, and she and Miss Morrill (Yankee as she is) have been devoting the whole time to the sick. Miss Carrie stays even at night as the soldiers seem to prefer her nursing to anyone else's, but Cousin Lucy is now quite sick, and we fear she has taken the fever.[29]

There was a young man, a Mr. McIllhaney from Alabama (who was ill with Bilious fever, whom I attended at the Hospital) that Cousin Lucy was afraid would take the typhoid fever if left in the hospital. She had him removed here to Charlie's old room upstairs, and, as Mother would not allow me to go to the hospital, I have been the nurse of this young man. He is so gentle and amiable that it is a pleasure to attend to his wants. He is much better now and I hope will soon be well.

I received a letter from Maggie last week who, though she was in very bad health, seemed to be in good spirits and enjoying Victor's company.

I received a letter from Mr. Butler, I think last Saturday, the first I have had. He was well and in better spirits than he has enjoyed since the commencement of this campaign.

I met a nice old man at the Delevan to whom I told the story of my want of a servant for Mr. Butler, and a few days since he came down and offered his services. Uncle Sam says he can wash and cook and will start for the camp in the morning with Mr. Holiday, and Mr. Butler will be relieved from his present office as cook, etc., which is as inelegant as disagreeable. So I will write this evening and send the letter by Uncle Sam.

We received a letter from Charlie last week, the first that has

29. The Delevan Hospital, also known as the "Mudwall," was adjacent to the railway depot and comprised one of the facilities of the Charlottesville General Hospital. See the introduction for more information on the Charlottesville General Hospital and on Confederate women's nursing efforts.

reached us since he left. He was then busy taking care of himself and smoking as he has nothing else to do, but another letter came from him saying that he has obtained a position as assistant to Colonel Petersham, commander of ordinance. He owed this principally to Col. Starkes's influence. He has made the acquaintance of Gen. Lowring and staff.

Sunday, father came home from Richmond, and had just succeeded in securing the appointment of aide-de-camp for Charlie in Greyson's Regiment that is going to Florida, and we have not yet learned whether he would prefer to keep his present post or resign it in favour of the one Father obtained for him.

I received in answer to my letter a short, cold, formal note from Dr. Mays last week giving me the information that I asked, telling me the Florida Regiment arrived in Virginia on the 22nd of July, and there was no chance for Mr. Butler's getting an office, and that all of his family, except the blind and the lame, were now in this State.

Whilst Father was in Richmond he learned that the Florida Regiment was stationed there, and went out to the Camp and saw Capt. Call, but Lieut. N. Butler and Sergeant L. Butler were absent, the latter young Gentleman was in some difficulty and was anticipating a duel: it seems he was ordered to make a man drill for punishment, and the soldier refused to obey orders, so he stuck a bayonet in him which caused a great commotion, and he left the company, and now has an office in another, and the prospect of a duel.

Father met Nick Butler on the street afterwards and he promised to come up to see us in a few days, and I hope he may come, for the first mark of kindness from one of Mr. Butler's relatives would be of some comfort to me.

Father thought there was some probability of Mr. Butler's obtaining an office if he should go to Richmond, either in his own Regiment or elsewhere, and I thought of writing to Mr. Nick, and getting him to write something definite to his Brother, and sending the letter to me so that I could forward it by private persons, but I concluded that if he did not care enough for his Brother to write without this reminder I would not trouble him.

Father received a letter from Cooper who left us Monday, more than a week ago, much to our regret, but he says he is well, and will be here on his way home in four weeks, so we are to some extent consoled as we are looking forward to seeing him again ere long.

Charlottesville. September 16, 1861

I have just finished reading *Muller's Life of Trust* which I have been reading for a month or two for it is a book that all through teaches the same lesson, and as I wish that lesson not to be forgotten I read it slowly, especially I wished it impressed on my mind as I cannot keep the book with me to refer to, for it is a book that Mr. Dinwiddie was so kind as to read a portion of it to me, and when he left Locust Hill he left it there for me to read.[30]

I have never before had anything to so impress me with the power and efficacy of prayer, not only in regard to spiritual but also to temporal blessings. It is the life of one who depended entirely upon God for his daily bread; what little he had he sold and gave to the poor. He refused to take any salary from his people but placed a box in his church where all who willed it might put what they wished. For some time he laboured in Bristol, and was often nearly brought to want. This he looked on as merely a trial of faith, but God never let him suffer for his faith was strong. He established a "Scriptual Knowledge Institution" for distributing Bibles, tracts, etc., and assisting missionaries at home and abroad. He established three Orphan Homes, all containing 1,150 orphans, besides assisting the poor and many other good works. All of these institutions he supported with funds given him in answer to prayer, for whenever he needed ought to carry on the work he prayed for it, believing it would be given him, not once or twice, but until his prayer was granted, and he always asked first whether it were God's will that he should carry out these works, and would not enter on them until he knew it was His will.

30. George Müller's autobiography, *The Life of Trust: Being A Narrative of the Lord's Dealings with George Müller*. Müller was an evangelist and reformer of orphanages in England.

Now ought not this to be the rule of life that all of us should adopt: to trust God for everything, and of that which He gives, give freely, and not look on ourselves as the owners of that which He gives but as only the stewards thereof, and then the more we ask, the more will He give us as long as we continue to dispose more freely of that which we have. And if God will give me grace I will make this my rule and walk by it so far as in me lieth and he will strengthen me to do so. (Levit. "That as not the refuse of the animals was offered us, so the best part of our time should be especially given to communion with the Lord."[31] I was by this stirred up afresh to early rising. By the grace of God I was enabled to begin the next day to rise earlier. How much time shall I allow for rest? No general rule can be given for this? Females being weaker in body require more sleep than males. Yet I learn that it is the opinion of medical men that a man in health does not require more than six or seven hours sleep and females no more than seven or eight hours. M.)

Charlottesville. October 15, 1861

A few days after I last wrote in this book, about the 18th of September, Mr. Butler came home, and found Charlie here who started to Florida that week, and we have heard nothing from him since, though he must have reached Fernandina long since, but I heard a few days since that Greyson was about to die.

Mr. Butler and Father went to Richmond together, and whilst he was away Mr. Butler went to York to see his brother where he found him and Cousin Lieut. Simpkins asleep, which amusement he found that they indulged in nearly all of the time, and left the work for Capt. Call to do. They had every comfort possible in Camp, and their fare was delightful, having fish, oysters, poultry, fruit, and game in abundance.

Mr. Butler tried very hard whilst in Richmond to get some appointment or, at least, an exchange of service, and, after being away a week,

31. This is a quote from George Müller, discussing Leviticus, in *A Narrative of Some of the Lord's Dealings with George Muller, Second Part, Fourth Edition* (London: J. Nisbet and Co., 1855), 296.

he returned home with a fond belief that Mr. Mallory and his relative, Mr. Cole (now chief of Johnson's staff) could do something for him, but it was a vain hope, and when the 5th of October arrived he has to set out for his camp again, which he did with anything but a good grace for he was in very low spirits, and dreaded the dreadful hardships of the western service very much. There is no hope of his getting another furlowe for the one he has was granted only because he had been quite sick, and was then unfit for service.

I received a few lines from him last week, written the day after he left me on Sunday. He was then in Lewisburgh and his spirits seemed to be more depressed than when he left for he had seen several of his company there who gave him a deplorable account of the condition of the company. I have not heard what movements the western army have made since the retreat of the enemy who, it is sayed, were forced from their positions by starvation, but I hope the army will descend from these bleak barren mountains, and go somewhere where they will not suffer so much from cold and hunger as they have heretofore.

Mrs. Glover has been quite ill for the last week but she is better now, and Mr. Glover arrived yesterday which has very much cheered her. I called yesterday to see how she was, and Major Glover sent me word that Mr. Butler arrived safely in camp just before he left.[32]

> "Tears idle tears, I know now what they mean,
> Tears from the depths of some devine despair,
> Arise to the heart, and tremble in the eye,
> When looking on these happy autumn fields,
> And thinking of the days that are no more."[33]

I have been drinking in the sweet air all day which feels as balmy and cheering as the first breeze of spring after gloomy and stormy winter, and one would be almost cheated in belief that it was spring's

32. Remainder of the page erased.

33. Alfred, Lord Tennyson, "Tears, Idle Tears," in *The Princess* (1847).

bright face that has come again after the dull cold days of rain and cloud that have preceded this did we not see a few seared leaves silently falling to their mother earth, and the groves and woods around us cloathed in their gaudy hues which, alas, is but a disguise of the deadness that lies in their hearts and chill which is curdling the blood in their veins.

The ground has been too wet and muddy all day for me to venture out or I should have been in the fields and woods securing the rich treasures of the season, but instead of this I spent most of the morning assisting Dear Aunt Lucy. The remainder of my time was occupied in knitting a glove for Mr. Butler, in which work I was so much interested, and in such haste to finish it that I took it with me in the afternoon when I went with Aunt Lucy to Uncle Ben's who has quite a settlement there of Alexandrians: Aunt Mary Hunter, Grandmother and her Daughters, Harriet and Mary. They all seemed very cheerful and bright, especially Grandmother who had completed her first wonderful stocking which was really quite a wonderful production.

Tuesday I received quite a long cheerful letter from Mr. Butler, and he seemed to hope for a battle in a few days as he expected to advance, as soon as they were provisioned, on the retreating army, but I fear this will not be done from what the papers say, and that instead both parties will retire to winter quarters. Oh, that we had attacked the enemy when they were in our power! It is true they had the advantage of us in numbers but our men very brave Southerners. Now that they have gone back to Gauley, what can we do?

We were cheered on Sunday last by hearing of the exploits of our wonderful iron clad steamer in the harbour of New Orleans, it having sunk one of the blockading vessels and run two aground.[34]

The army at Manassas are advancing and retiring so often we can scarcely keep account of their movements, but the last news was that they had retired to Manassas, and that the enemy were advancing. This

34. The Battle of the Head of Passes (October 12, 1861) was a naval battle that resulted in a Confederate victory. A Confederate mosquito fleet and the ironclad CSS *Manassas* attacked Union blockade vessels, which fled their blockade position.

gives us hope of a speedy battle, but we have been looking for one there so long that we scarcely know what to expect.

Mollie has been sick with bilious fever at Mr. Scott's in Fredericksburgh for a week or more, and Aunt Lucy has, of course, been very uneasy, and this evening she heard that Mr. Daniel was coming in a few days for little Sady, and this distressed Aunt Lucy very much, and, as she is at Farmington, we will bring her home in the morning.

Locust Hill. October 21, 1861

This has been a very pleasant day to me, the first that I have been able to walk out, so, in order to make up for lost time, I started out before Aunt Lucy's early breakfast in search of chestnuts, accompanied by my cousins, Merry and Harp. We went through the little piece of woodland that surrounds the school house, and after spending half an hour or more we returned ladened with chestnuts, bright leaves, and berrys, and some moss of which I made, or rather filled, a hanging basket in which I planted a dew plant that I brought from Farmington on Sunday morning, for we were detained until then by untoward circumstances.

Mr. Anderson and Mr. Massie went with us, and we found Mother and Walter there, and in the evening Mrs. Bankhead and Miss Susan Michie called, the latter young lady made many neat and appropriate remarks which were much to the point.

Mother sayed that since my departure from home a letter had been received from Charlie who had Gaundis very badly ever since his arrival in Florida, and that Mr. Samuel Butler had sent his servant to attend on him.[35] Gen. Greyson was ill with consumption, and he (Charlie) was then acting as Adjutant Gen., and his opinion of the country coincided with Father's in thinking that it bore a strong resemblance to his Satanic Majesty.

Fernandina was threatened with an attack and the women and children were leaving the place, and, as all of Mr. Butler's servants were there and he thought some hope of his getting an office if he were in the

35. Butler is most likely referring to jaundice.

State, he urged him to come on, but I suppose it will be impossible for him to do so as he had already exhausted every means of obtaining a release from his company.

Uncle Merry was so good as to bring me a letter from Camp Defiance, Lewis Mountain, at dinner time. Mr. Butler was well and cheerful, and seemed quite content with his lot in life, rather enjoying himself than otherwise on the top of the Mountain, surrounded by the wild and beautiful scenery, whose loveliness was enhanced by the rich glowing sunsets and the brilliant foliage of the trees. The enemy had retreated some distance, Lee still inactive, and Floyd was no one knew where.

I had scarcely time to read my letter for Merry hurried me so to go with him after chestnuts. We made a plan to go last evening and to join the Watsons at Dr. Woods's.

We started out in good time and with a pleasant party and cool bracing air. I enjoyed it exceedingly. Merry and Willie Woods climbed the trees, and it came as near to my idea of the happiness experienced by Fleda when Carleton thrashed the trees for her (only far less in degree) as anything I had witnessed, though I fear Merry did not enjoy it much for he and Helen had to avoid each other, and he is still under the influence a little.

We did not find a great many chestnuts as the Servants had been in search of them all of the day before, so we went after grapes, and found a great many, after which we started home, having greatly enjoyed the afternoon.

Locust Hill. October 28, 1861

This day, one week ago, a battle was fought on the banks of the Potomac, near Lewisburgh, in which glorious victory was gained by the brave patriots of the South. 600 prisoners were taken and are now in Richmond, 300 were drowned, and, altogether, with the shot and wounded, 1200 men were lost by the North. Various state the numbers of the enemy, some say 10,000, others more, some less, but of this we know: the late Colonel, now General, Evans withstood the enemy with four imperfect Regiments, and with this force obtained a great victory.[36]

Yet so, that victory seems but too dearly bought, and in place of rejoicing it fills me with sorrow for many others, and I believe the Confederacy lost more than was gained for there fell one of the truest bravest patriots that all the land contained. On that day our Dear lamented friend, Mr. Cooper, fell, he so gentle to his friends, so generous to his foes, with heart burning to serve his country, and mark out his nation's freedom.[37] Not one harsh word against our oppressors ever escaped his lips, not when he was willing to yield up to utter desolation his beloved State and to witness

> "The wild Mother scream
> O'er her femishing brood."

ere he would submit to the tyrants.

I know not what the world may say, I have not seen whether he is applauded for his notable deeds or whether he is passed over "to fame unknown," but this I know: that none who has known him can ever forget, and that there is an enduring monument in the hearts of all claiming to be his friends. But one sad thought will arise for we cannot say, "Yet in heaven we hope to meet him," we cannot say this without feeling, alas! How faint that hope.

36. The Battle of Ball's Bluff was fought in Loudoun County, Virginia, on October 21, 1861; it was a Confederate victory. Brigadier General Charles P. Stone and Colonel Edward Baker led the Union forces, and Brigadier General Nathan G. Evans led the Confederates. Two thousand Union forces were engaged against sixteen hundred Confederate forces.

37. Cooper was a soldier who was nursed back to health at the Wood home in August 1861. Butler repeatedly calls Cooper "noble" and "honourable"; for an extended description of Cooper, see Butler's diary, August 6, 1861.

This sad, sad, news I have just heard today, and yesterday we heard that Mr. Dinwiddie was very ill in Lewisburgh with fever. Oh! How the dark clouds are thickening around us.

Charlottesville. November 7, 1861

On Friday last, Snowden came to Locust Hill for me, and sayed that Mr. Butler had arrived that morning and sent for me, so Snowden, Harper, the gun, and I, started off in a rickety little buggy drawn by a small bobtailed horse who seemed to enter into the spirit of getting home before the storm, and owing to his kind exertions we reached home just as it commenced raining.[38]

Mr. Butler was on his way to Richmond as he was bearer of Dispatches to Gens. Lee and Wise, and had procured a furlough of 25 days on condition that Wise would sign it. So the next morning he left, met with an accident, or rather the train did, for there was a collision and the cars were much injured, but no one hurt. The train was detained so long that it did not reach Richmond until four in the morning. However, he went to see Wise next day, Sunday as it was, found him looking pale and thin and very much like a ghost, and, by the way, he says like a very wicked old ghost, but he had no power at all to grant furloughs as he is not now in command.

Mr. Butler saw Lydia in the afternoon and took her to see Mrs. Cole.

The next morning he called on Gen. Lee before he was up and got him to sign the furlough when he was about half asleep. So after his six o'clock call he came up home and I met him at the depot, for he thought it probable when he left that he would be sent back to Western Virginia with Dispatches and perhaps would not return, but was so fortunate as to be able to start for Florida the day after he reached this place on Wednesday. I was very glad he went and had expressed my anxiety for him to go in a letter a few days before he came, and he says that is what made him make the attempt to leave the West. Until then he had been content with his hard lot and thought it strange I should have been so

38. Snowden was her younger brother (b. 1847).

fickle for in the letter I had written just before this last I had exhorted him to be satisfied and remain where he was. But I did not then know that the western service would continue so inglorious. However, after the retreat of Yankee forces to Gauley Bridge, I concluded that nothing but disgrace would be gained by remaining and no good would be done either his country or himself, and then cold winter was advancing, and he is totally unfit to stand the climate. Those reasons combined with the state in which Florida is now in, with an attack from the Northern armada, made me very anxious that he should be there, for I think his duty is first to defend his own State, and besides his affairs need attention there. If Mr. Butler can succeed in securing an office that will release him from his present service, he will remain in Florida, and, if everything be quiet enough, he wishes me to join him there though I fear that will be impossible. Mr. Cole offered him the use of his house, servants, carriage, and horses, for the winter, but, of course, we would not like to take advantage of his kindness.

Father heard from Charlie today. He was then in New Orleans when he wrote; had gone thither with one of Greyson's sons to take care of the old General's body, and had just attended his funeral which was conducted with much pomp and parade as he was both a Catholic and a man of military distinction, but I suppose Charlie has returned to Florida some time since.[39]

I am fearing that my journal will soon become a record of deaths, for, after the sad loss we have so lately sustained which I mentioned a few pages back, I must now speak of the loss of another equally dear Friend. Since these two have been taken I feel as if there were no certainty who would be the next victim to this barbarous war that is being waged against us—two of the men that I admired most.

39. Brigadier General John Breckinridge Grayson died on October 21, 1861, in Tallahassee, Florida. He attended West Point and served in the Mexican-American War. After resigning his post in the U.S. Army to join the Confederacy, he soon died of tuberculosis. He did not fight in a single battle of the Civil War.

On Monday last, Harmon Dinwiddie's remains were brought home. He died in Lewisburgh after a short but severe illness of typhoid pneumonia. But as much more for the heavy loss which I and the world have sustained, I do not grieve for him, for his life was such that there can be no doubt that he is among the blessed, and that education which he so longed to complete will be completed perfectly. He had always expressed a willingness, almost amounting to a desire, to die, though he was too good to long for death if there was any work to do for Christ here, for he was ever longing to be able to do more in the great cause, and would like to have fallen on the battle field serving his country, but he was resigned, I know, to go in whatever way it pleased his Maker to call him. He was endowed by nature with a very handsome person, and, pleading the cause of Christ, his face would so beam with intelligence and be lit up by feeling that he looked as though he were inspired.

He was very intelligent, brave, noble, with refined poetic feelings, and sensitive and diffident so that he was often thought cold and reserved, but he seemed not so to me, and I think he had a warm heart and deep affections that were often wounded by less refined natures. He had so strict a sense of Duty that he was rather uncharitable when others went astray but he was young and would have overcome all of this. I once sayed and still think him the most perfect character I ever met with. I could not see then but that he was perfect, and, since then, these slight faults have been pointed out to me.

His sensitive nature had rendered him a little morbid and he felt that no one cared for him, but during his illness he talked much of Aunt Lucy and Uncle Merry and of me, spoke very affectionately, and when he was delirious he would tell them in his ravings of the cap I had sent him and sayed they must take good care of it for Mrs. Butler made it. How great a work would he have done had he been spared, though he was not happy and now all is bliss and joy with him, and now I feel that his life and conversation have, by God's grace, made a lasting impression that will help me to lead a better life, and doubt not that through his means the seeds have been sown in the hearts of others that will spring into everlasting life.

November 12, 1861

I have just read a lively bright little autumn piece with all of its bright hopes for the future and rich pleasure of the present, and though the chill blast would sweep by, and the leaves were falling thick and fast, and many a skeleton branch stretched forth, stripped of its glory, yet a close observer could even there see the little bud which was waiting for spring to blossom forth, and as I read of these things and the hopes and joys of innocent hearts, it all seems a bright vision caught from another world, and my eyes would fill when the thought would come that none of these is for me. We live now with no Earthly hope, no future. We live from day to day, knowing not what a day or an hour may bring forth, waiting to hear perhaps that he who is nearest us has fallen by the hand of disease or in the battle field, or of some great battle where hundreds of our dear boys are

> "Left on the ground overpowered
> The weary to sleep and the wounded to die."[40]

Thoughts of conquests do not enter our minds. All we hope for is to maintain our liberty by a mighty struggle, we know not how long, we fear for many years may it last, but yield, that will we never.

In the midst of this our sorrow, sad indeed would be our fate if we did not not trust in a higher power who we know can deliver us from the hands of all our enemys, and if we did not have a hope in Heaven and a future which is eternity.

Sunday we were sent for by the Maurys to attend the funeral of poor little Jesse who died the day before, after much suffering, with scarlet fever. The family were all much grieved and they will sadly miss the sweet child. How fast is every house becoming the house of mourning.

40. A reference to Thomas Campbell, "The Soldier's Dream" (1804).

Charlottesville. November 15, 1861

Yesterday was my 20th birthday. It seems strange that it should be so, for I still feel like a child, and have not grown much in this long time, and do not feel at all like a married lady of twenty.

I wonder where I shall be when twenty years more have passed, whether I shall have then happiness or misery, or whether I shall be in existence or not, for this latter I care not much.

The day passed without adventure, though I was not as busy as I have recently been for in the three preceding days I had made eight dresses. This day was appointed and has been kept as a solemn day of prayer and fasting.[41] Mr. Meade preached and exhorted us to humble ourselves and think not that we were the favoured of God for righteousness.

I went to see Mrs. Brogan. She seemed to be comfortably supporting herself by sewing. She told me a long story about the Earl of Glengal of Ireland whose family name was Butler. She had been a tenant on his estate and sayed she was sure that he and Mr. Butler were of the same family, and I remember hearing him speak of relatives there who belonged to the nobility.

I have no room now but have to stay with Lizzie and her apartment is always full of people, and five persons in one room disputing is not propitious to writing. I have to close without saying what I wish invariably.

"Rebels! 'Tis a holy name!
The name our fathers bore,
When battling in the cause of right,
Against the tyrant in his might,
In the dark days of yore.

"Rebels! 'Tis our family name!
Our Father, Washington,

41. Jefferson Davis declared nine official days of fasting throughout the war; see "Diary" nn. 19, 52, and 75.

Was the Arch Rebel in the fight
And gave the name to us:—a right
Of father to the son."[42]

Locust Hill. January 30, 1862

Time has flown rapidly and some of it happily, though much sadness and sorrow I have also felt since I have last written here, and each day I would that I would seize the passing events, at least a reminder of them, ere they had all flown forever, but ever and anon some duty or pleasure would call me off. Now I have a bright fire, Mollie has gone to bed and will soon be wrapt in the arms of Morpheus, so I am alone, and at liberty to spend my time in any way most agreeable to my fancy. I could not find a fitter time to resume my diary, and I think I had best revert to the time that has intervened since my last writing.

One of the most interesting events to me was Texy's entering into the Holy estate of matrimony. Many were doubtful who would be favoured of her admirers for there were four of them who seemed as uncertain on the subject as disinterested persons, and she received several letters just before, and immediately after, her marriage that would never have been written had the writer known of the step she was taking. It was near the first of Dec., I have forgotten the exact date, that Capt. S. Preston came to claim his bride.

It was quite a surprise to us for she had kept the matter quite private as she was determined that she would not have the same accident happen as occurred to Miss Tiny a short time since, that is, make all things ready and public, and the groom fail to arrive. But, true to his word, he came, and quite a handsome pair they made: she in her simple muslin, the uniform for brides during war. All of her female friends were present, a few Old Gentlemen, and 2 youthful ones, and quite a pleasant evening it was.

I have succeeded in getting up quite a superstition about Mr. Butler's returning home. I am always sure for a day or two before he arrives that

42. Anonymous, "Rebels," n.d.

he will soon come, and I have concluded that he would be home in time to be at Texy's wedding. He had been away a month, and I had no reason to believe that he would return from Florida for I did not hear from him whilst he was away, and I was very much disappointed at his non-arrival, but a day or two after, when I was not expecting it, he came.

Lydia came home for she was just recovering from measles. She soon recuperated and we had a pleasant time in spite of the war, though it would throw its grim shadow across the hearth sometimes.

We were very busy preparing Christmas gifts, and St. Nick seemed more bountiful than usual for he visited every one in the house with two exceptions. I had quite a handsome pair of slippers for Mr. Butler but, as they could not be finished sooner, I was promised that they should be sent early Christmas morning, but they did not arrive until every one had emptied and enjoyed the contents of their stockings, and nothing was seen for him, and he must have felt rather neglected, but presently the slippers came, and he seemed perfectly delighted.

The Farmingtonians and Girls from the Maury's dined with us, and Mrs. Glover and several of Mr. Butler's friends came to our Eggnog on Christmas evening. The friends were all members of the University Volunteers which had just been disbanded. They were Capt. Crane, a very pleasant, amiable Gentleman who, it is sayed, never lost his temper during the campaign in Western Virginia; Mr. McCorby whom we knew last session; and Mr. Misher, one of the most celebrated men for ugliness that I know of, and his voice exceeds his appearance. He would take the most ungainly postures possible, but, for all, he is sayed to be intelligent, and good, and a man of fine character.

Aunt Mary asked us to come to see her during the holidays, and bring some of our friends, so Friday morning we got a carriage and went out. Mr. McCorby and Capt. Crane were our friends. Soon Betty and Nannie, and Mr. Strange, Mrs. McKenney, and Mr. Massie, and Merry, and several, or rather, a good many others arrived.

We spent the day in agreeable conversation and the evening in games and tableaux. The games were only introduced between the scenes. Betty made a beautiful Imogene. Lizzie impersonated Lady Percy, with Mr. Strange as Hotspur, and he really bears a striking resemblance to Harry as he appears in one of the Farmington pictures, but it was an unfortunate remark of mine that it was appropriate for Mr. Strange to take that character as nothing would induce him to fight for his country but a good office and an easy time. Nannie looked sweet as a novice, and Cousin Lou made a fine Lady Abbess. Lydia and I both appeared in the same scenes that we did some years ago at home.[43]

We went home the next morning after having been very pleasantly entertained. Lydia, though nearly broken down for she was not very well, could not resist the invitation of Emma and Bertha Rives who came for her that morning, and she remained with them until the next day.

That evening, notwithstanding it was Saturday, Miss Carrington had a party which was not very pleasant as she invited fully grown girls of various kinds and boys from the University of sixteen to talk to them, and, as this was called a surprise party, Lizzie sayed that they might surprise her Monday evening, and, though she began to regret it, yet she could not retract.

Mr. Butler intended leaving for Florida on Monday but Mrs. Glover succeeded in persuading him to wait until the next day.

Quite a large company assembled Monday evening, all of the girls that we visit and several others besides. Mr. Adams, one of Mr. Butler's friends at school who was a sick soldier, came with the two younger Singletons; a Dr. Walker, hospital surgeon, who was a very intelligent South Carolinian, and a host of boys from the University, that none

43. According to a footnote in the original diary text, a program of the tableaux was found in her papers and included in this copy of her diary: "Scene 1: Magic Mirror (The wizard shows the Knight his 'ladye faire'); Scene 2: The Duenna (a Spanish lady while receiving a lecture from her duenna hands a note to her lover); Scene 3 (from Peveril of the Peak): Duke of Buckingham and Fenella (played by Lucy Wood and Waddy Butler); Scene 4 (from David Copperfield): David suddenly appears at his Aunt's house; Scene 5: The Coquette (The lady shows favor first to one lover and then the other); Scene 6: Getting in a scrape and getting out; Scene 7: Auld Robin Grey (Auld Robin is 'gude man' to Jennie. Jamie returns to claim his Jennie. Played by Lizzie Wood and Robt. Cooper); Scene 8: Feast of Roses (Nourmahal brings Namouna the flowers to weave the magic wreath)."

of us knew and whose acquaintance we did not make. Some of Lydia's friends danced a while, and spent the rest of the evening listening to Kate's and Lydia's music, and drinking eggnog.

This was the last of the Christmas entertainments, and with it fled all that made us bright and merry then, for we were buoyed up by false and extravagant hopes of peace from the interference of England in our behalf, and the friends who were gathered around us were all soon scattered.

Tuesday morning Mr. Butler again started for Florida, and with no hopes of return as he expected to enlist for the war, but I have been very fortunate so far in hearing from him, for I have received three letters from him which, though sad, were yet great comforts to me.

About the 10th of January, I came here to Locust Hill on horseback with Snowden to assist dear Aunt Lucy in her many cares, for Uncle Merry had been ill for nearly a month. He had just commenced to enjoy himself as a member of the Legislature in the Lower House in Richmond, when he was taken sick, and remained so for some time, with a carbuncle. When he thought that he was nearly well, he came home, and has been very ill ever since, and both he and Aunt Lucy have almost ceased to hope for his recovery, but, blessed be the name of God, for such patience and resignation as they show.

I assist, and most of the time do all the housekeeping, and instruct and take care of Mollie.

Locust Hill. February 5, 1862

Last Friday I received a note from home telling me that Ward's brother Nick had come from Yorktown to see me.[44] I was much pleased at hearing this as I always admired and liked him as an acquaintance, and, now that he was something nearer, of course the feeling deepened.

Accordingly, the next morning, I started for the station, in spite of the rain and frightful roads, on horseback. I had no escort on the cars, and Mr. Abel of Charlottesville undertook to play the agreeable, and, not knowing that I was a married lady, commenced teasing me about

44. Ward was her husband, Waddy.

the school boys here. As he seemed to enjoy the idea I did not undeceive him. Then Mr. Sheffey of Staunton introduced himself and mistook me for a school girl in my childish straw hat. He then inquired how many beaux I had and what I did with them. I replied I had but one and had married him, a short time since.

Mr. Nick dined with me, but in the afternoon he went into the country after his cousin, Ebby, and they, with Major and Mrs. Glover, spent the evening with us. Mr. Nick went to church with me the next day, and, as our church was closed, we heard Dr. Hoge preach, rather an ordinary sermon for him. Brother was obliged to leave Monday morning as his furlough had expired. I had no opportunity of conversing with him as I had wished and consequently I made a very poor impression, that of being cold and indifferent, though I was far from feeling so.

I had promised to return to my duties Monday morning, and, though the snow was falling fast and was a foot deep already, I was determined that it should not deter me. As I found out from Ebby Butler that a cousin of his and also of Mr. Butler's was at the Farish house, I promised to call on her before leaving town. I ordered the sleigh and at Mr. Watson's request I went to the Cochrans' for Mary Woodson who, since her Father is dead, had to go on business to the Court House, to which place I took her, and bade her farewell as she left for South Carolina to-day. I then called on Mrs. Van, in whose favour I was not at all prepossessed.

The station was crowded by every description of persons, especially by very disagreeable descriptions, and most of the masculine portion of the assembly seemed to have been trying to dispose of as much ardent spirit as possible. I fortunately met with Mr. J. Warwick Woods who very kindly took care of me until my arrival at Woodville. I found no one waiting for me, and Cousin Charlie secured me a seat in Willie Wood's sleigh.

I have commenced my pupil in the French language since my return, and think that after I kept her in nearly all day she will progress finely in all of her studies.[45]

45. She refers to Mollie Anderson as her pupil.

Yesterday Joe Cross was taken sick with a chill but this evening he became violently ill. Perfectly frantic, Dr. White was sent for, and Cousin Bob Price (who has just arrived from Missouri) was requested to come from Mr. Maury's. Both doctors are now with him and he is pronounced very dangerously ill with congestive fever. What sorrow will come next? It seemed enough and as much as could be borne already, but may the ruler of all give us strength, and hope, and faith.

February 19, 1862

Each day everything assumes a gloomier aspect, both at home and abroad, and accounts of our sad disasters come thick and fast.

On Monday, more than a week since, we heard of the capture of Roanoke Island. Various reports arrived until we at length learned that, with the exception of 2 or 3 companies, all of the Wise Legion were forced, after having gallantly fought and exhausted all of their ammunition, to surrender to an overwhelming force that completely surrounded them, but this victory was not gained without great loss of life on the part of the enemy, and it is sayed that we lost only seventeen, among whom the brave and noble Captains Wise and Coles fell, gallantly fighting. General Wise was ill at the time and consequently escaped the hands of the invaders who next took undisturbed possession of Edington, and we are expecting daily to hear of their having taken Weldon, and thus cutting off all communication with the South.[46]

I became so much excited on the subject a few days ago that I determined at once to start for Florida, but "not knowing the way," and having no escort, I have given up the idea. I still hear from Florida quite frequently, and it would be very sad to me if this source of happiness was taken away.

46. The Battle of Roanoke Island (February 7–8, 1862) was a Union victory. A Union force of about seventy-five hundred men, led by Brigadier General Ambrose Woodside, suffered approximately three hundred casualties.

Next came news that the Rubicons had taken possession of Florence in North Alabama, and a great quantity of valuable Government Stores were destroyed to prevent their possessing themselves of them.[47]

Fort Henry was given up to the Yankees.[48] And we heard for several days of dreadful fighting at Fort Donelson, and we had several times repulsed and put the enemy to flight with great slaughter, but yesterday it was reported, and today confirmed, that the enemy had been reinforced, and came in such overwhelming numbers that the Fort fell, and it is sayed Gens. Pillar, Buckner, and Johnson made prisoners.[49] Floyd escaped, and Nashville has been given up on condition that private property shall not be disturbed. We are almost in despair and all hopes of foreign aid have at length come to an end.[50]

Uncle Merry is as ill as possible, and poor Joe, after having nearly recovered, has relapsed, and is quite sick.

Monday I received some comfort. Maggie has written at last, and Sallie Street wrote today.

Late, late, so late, and dark the night and chill.

Locust Hill. February 27, 1862

Our first President, and it is feared by many our last, was inaugurated on Saturday, the 22nd, and nature seemed to weep over the

47. Florence was a key strategic stronghold as it is located on a major transportation artery: the Tennessee River.

48. The Battle of Fort Henry (February 6, 1862) was a major Union victory as it gave the Union increased access to the Tennessee River. Both sides withstood a low number of casualties: approximately forty for the Union and seventy-nine for the Confederacy.

49. The Battle of Fort Donelson (February 11–16, 1862) was a decisive Union victory led by Brigadier General Ulysses S. Grant and Flag Officer A. H. Foote. It resulted in approximately fifteen thousand Confederate casualties (compared to approximately two thousand Union casualties). The victory, coupled with Grant and Foote's previous victory at Fort Henry (see "Diary" n. 48), allowed Union passage on the Tennessee and Cumberland Rivers, leaving the state of Tennessee, and the greater South, more vulnerable to Union invasion.

50. Butler references the prospect of British and French recognition of the Confederacy.

useless and inappropriate form and cast a deeper gloom, as its clouds seemed to forebode darker days to come.[51]

For the last week we have been vacillating between hope and fear for the reports of our sad losses have been contradicted several times, but at last all of the bad news has been positively confirmed, and Nashville is even occupied by the enemy, never to be abandoned again. And now that treachery and cowardice seem to have arisen in our land, hope is dying out, and we have brought ourselves to look the worst bravely in the face, and think of what we shall do when the Yankee tyrant reigns supreme, and grinds us to dust by insult and wrong. If I were a man, no such thought would dare enter my mind, but I, being merely a woman, must sit still, with my weak sisters, for fear of doing aught unwomanly, and see 7000 men surrender as they did at Donelson, a deed that women would have blushed to own, and a deed that makes us weep to feel that such men are our countrymen. Oh, may the black flag soon wave over the land, and fight to the death, or live victorious, be the watchword! Pure cowardice would be enough to make *men* fight now for if we do not win, what would life be: a useless burden when honour, happiness, wealth are gone, and disgrace and oppression descend upon us.

The inhabitants of Suffolk are rapidly leaving with their servants and moveable property as an attack may be made at any moment. A battle is daily expected along the Potomac line, and we have only a disorganized and nearly disbanded army to meet the foe.

Uncle Merry and Joe continue very ill. Tomorrow is appointed a day of solemn prayer and fasting.[52] Oh, may our merciful Father bless us and hear in pity the cries that we send up to his throne.

This was a clear cold day and, for the sake of the exercise, Mollie and I played a game of ball with the boys.

51. Jefferson Davis was inaugurated on February 18, 1861, in Montgomery, Alabama (the first capital of the Confederacy). Butler is most likely referring to his second inauguration in Richmond (the second capital of the Confederacy).

52. Davis declared nine official days of fasting throughout the war; see "Diary" nn. 19, 41, and 75.

Locust Hill. March 3, 1863

Yesterday Uncle Merry was much worse and we did not expect him to live until this morning but he has been spared to us this long, and he revived a little this morning, but tonight new and alarming symptoms have manifested themselves. His pulse is so weak that it can scarcely be felt at all, and of course our hopes are now very faint. He longs for the hour when he can shake off his mortal coil, and when he can leave off the corruptible and put on incorruption.

Joe seems to be slowly recovering.

Our public affairs still assume a dark and lowering aspect, but no new disaster has fallen us except our men are turning traitors. The Hon. John M. Boots, with a dozen citizens of Richmond, has been arrested on the charge of High Treason. It seems that Miss Moton recognized two persons as Northern men. They were arrested and have proven to be spies, and papers were found in their possession implicating Boots, etc. Richmond is in great fear and agitation. The City has been declared under martial law and all drinking establishments have closed and disorder of all kinds put a stop to. The City has been drafted from sixteen to twenty to form a guard, a bodyguard to the President.

Mr. Tunstall returned today and gave us the news. Lizzie Maury came up Friday and she and I walked over to my home to see Cousin Alice on Saturday evening. She went home this morning through all of the rain as her Uncle Bob ordered her to go. She is such a pleasant agreeable child that all of the boys were quite fascinated with her.

Locust Hill. March 13, 1862

For some time past everything here has been too exciting and sad for me to write.

On Wednesday, 5th of March, Dear Uncle Merry passed from Earth to Heaven, not merely willing to leave this vale of tears, but happy to go, for he sayed that all was bright before him.

The next day his remains were committed to earth, and, deep as was the affliction there was almost a shout of triumph in every heart when we remembered that God in mercy and wisdom did not forsake him after his having spent so many years in the service of the world, but continued to strive with him until he became one of the band of the unfaithful. Today a number of letters came directed to the Hon. M. L. Anderson. They had been in Richmond and were just forwarded. A day or two since, Aunt Lucy received lists of resolutions taken in both Houses of the Legislature of Virginia expressing their grief and sympathy.

As I have been the only one with Aunt Lucy I have had a great deal to do in order to trouble her as little as possible for we have very few servants, and, of them, Sallie is sick, and Mary Jones has been taken away, and we are all kept busy. I think perhaps it is best for Aunt Lucy as it diverts her mind from her sorrow.

Everyone is excited at the militia draft, and it sayed that Letcher has committed fraud in ordering all of the militia, and it is thought he will be impeached.[53] During the last few days we have continued to receive accounts of the wonderful exploits of the Virginia, alias the Merrimac, in Hampton Roads, and of the great execution we did at Newport News.[54]

Another victory is reported to have been gained by Gen. Price in Arkansas but Gen. McCullough and several others of distinction fell. The Northern army claim this victory also and I do not know which side to believe.[55] Johnson has certainly evacuated Manassas and fallen back to Gordonville and the Stars and Stripes now wave over Centreville.

I was much startled this evening when Merry read out with other items of news that St. Marys and Fernandina had been taken by the Yankees as Mr. Butler was in Fernandina when I last heard from him, but the paper elsewhere stated that the place had been evacuated. So I suppose that all the damage the foe did us was to render us penniless.

53. From early 1862 there was discussion of enacting a universal conscription act. At the end of March, Davis issued a message to Congress advocating conscription. On April 16, 1862, the Confederacy passed the first conscription act in United States history.

54. The Battle of Hampton Roads (Battle of the Ironclads) was an inconclusive naval battle fought on March 8–9, 1862, off the coast of Virginia. The USS *Monitor* was pitted against the CSS *Virginia;* this marked the first engagement of ironclads. The Union suffered approximately four hundred casualties, the Confederacy twenty-five.

55. The Battle of Pea Ridge was fought in Benton County, Arkansas (March 6–8, 1862); it resulted in a Union victory. Confederate brigadier generals Benjamin McCulloch and James McQueen McIntosh were killed in the battle.

Charlottesville. May 2, 1862

When I last attempted to give a feeble account of surrounding events of interest to me, we were just recovering from the sudden shock we received by the fall of Fort Donelson, and were fearing and trembling at the movements of Johnson, but, since, we have learned to believe the retreat of our army from Manassas the greatest achievement we have yet made for, when the enemy reached our old encampment and found nothing, they were completely puzzled as to what it meant, and all of their plans disconcerted.

We were much cheered a few weeks since by our great victory in which we obtained New Corinth, at the Battle of Shiloh, though we lost one of our first commanders, Gen. Sidney Johnston; but we hope much from Beauregard who now has command of the western forces.[56]

About the first of April the enemy under Gen. McClellan landed a large force on the Peninsular and all of the army of the Potomac, but a small remnant, were ordered to Yorktown. Both parties entrenched themselves and we were daily expecting a tremendous battle, but for the last week we have believed this a delusion which the enemy made so that they might attack other points, and only constant skirmishing is kept up, as inglorious as it is dangerous.[57]

Fredericksburgh fell without a struggle.[58]

Nearly two weeks since we were expecting daily to be left within the enemy's lines as Jackson was retreating before a superior force. Sunday,

56. The Battle of Shiloh (April 6–7, 1862) was a Union victory. This was a particularly costly battle for both sides: Approximately 13,000 Union soldiers were killed, wounded, or missing, and approximately 10,700 Confederate soldiers were killed, wounded, or missing. Confederate brigadier general Albert Sidney Johnston died in the battle.

57. The Siege of Yorktown (April 5–May 4, 1862) set Union major general George McClellan against the Confederacy's Major General John B. Magruder and General Joseph Johnston; it was inconclusive.

58. The Battle of Fredericksburg was not fought until December 1862 (Confederate victory). Butler is likely referring to the occupation of northern Virginia and the concentration of skirmishes in this area. Fredericksburg, being equidistant from both the capitals of Washington, D.C., and Richmond, was a battle site twice during the war (the Second Battle of Fredericksburg was fought in May 1863 and was a Union victory).

the 21st of April, wagons of commissary stores, sick soldiers, refugees, all crowded in town all day through the rain which gave me a chill to look at it.

The armies were in a few miles of Staunton.

Then commenced excitement, some persons packed their trunks, others only talked. And I, after hearing Texy's account, was almost frantic with excitement, though I did try to be cool, for I had no idea of being left in the enemy's lines, and I knew not what to do. Jackson was reinforced very soon, and the excitement somewhat subsided, though a great many persons went away and are still leaving for Lynchburg, most of them. Among the rest was Mr. Frank Smith and family from Alexandria. I knew Mary Smith very well when I was smaller than I am now, and had just renewed our acquaintance, and I regretted much it was broken off so soon.

Our last great blow, I think the heaviest we have yet had to sustain, was the loss of New Orleans. The whole affair was so disastrous and disgraceful that it strikes every Southerner to the heart, and the gallant noble conduct of Mayor Monroe is all that we can look upon without trembling with mortification and rage.[59]

To return to my own personal affairs. I came home about the middle of March intending to return to Aunt Lucy after a visit of a week but I was detained by various things for two weeks when Mr. Butler came from Florida. Just as he had succeeded in raising a company, all of the troops were ordered to leave the State, so he disbanded his company, and, as he was up the St. John's River, he cut across the country en route for Virginia.

He brought some very peculiar presents: a beautiful little rifle, a pair of duelling pistols, and a knife.

The weather was for a while pleasant and Lydia, Aunt Anne, Mr.

59. On April 18, 1862, the Union commenced bombardment of the forts on the lower Mississippi River south of New Orleans, the Confederacy's largest city and former powerhouse of the antebellum slave economy. Eleven days later, on April 29, the city was captured by the Union.

Butler, and I, and the children spent one day most charmingly at Cochran's pond, fishing, shooting, reading, etc.

After a visit of two weeks, he left for Yorktown to join the Florida regiment there.

I am still here as everything is so unsettled that I know not at what moment I shall have to take up my line of march for I am determined not to remain in the enemy's lines as long as the Confederacy stands.

Charlottesville. May 6, 1862

Dark are the clouds and but little is the sunshine that beams on us now. Some days we hope a little but the next all of our hopes are dashed.

Yesterday we received a catalogue of events of startling interest and importance. The great battle near Corinth had already begun.[60] Savannah has declared that under no circumstances will she surrender. A great portion of Jackson's army were at Mechum's River yesterday when they received orders to march immediately for Staunton. Many of them had taken off their socks to wash them. They sent up shouts of joy at the order to march, hung their wet socks on their bayonets, threw their shoes in the wagons, and marched off gaily, barefooted.

Yorktown has been evacuated, our large guns all spiked, why we know not, nor do we know the destination of the army, though it is thought it has gone to defend Richmond. Norfolk has been evacuated, and the Navy Yard shipping, and all public stores destroyed.

Texy, Dr. Harrold, and myself are going on horseback to Farmington this afternoon after the cars come, if we not hear of any fresh misfortunes.

Charlottesville. May 9, 1862

We received dispatches yesterday that there had been fighting, and it was still continued on the Peninsular. The papers gave accounts of three battles that had taken place since Monday, with much loss on both

60. The Siege of Corinth (Miss.) began on April 29, 1862.

sides.[61] The enemy met our retreating forces and attacked them, and in one skirmish they were three times repulsed, but, as soon as they see any danger, they retire to the protection of their gun boats. Only Longstreet's and Stuart's divisions have been engaged, but a general engagement seems inevitable.

Texy went to Richmond this morning as Capt. Preston telegraphed for her to meet him there as he would be there with his company. We have heard of many who have been killed and wounded. Among the rest, Capt. Bennett Taylor has received a slight wound. I, of course, feel very anxious and depressed but do not think Mr. Butler was in the engagement. God help this our dear Country for everything looks quite doubtful now.

The cars this morning brought us the good news that Jackson had defeated the foe in two battles in the Valley.

Charlottesville. May 17, 1862

We receive many false reports that it is quite amusing to see the different and contradictory ones that I myself give in these pages. Some days since I mentioned that three battles had been fought in the army of the Peninsular, but it had proved to be only one, and that a severe one with very heavy losses on both sides, and, though we were the victors, yet so many fell that we could not triumph.[62]

I waited and watched most anxiously to hear from Mr. Butler, though I did not believe that he had been in the engagement as the papers stated that only Longstreet's and Stuart's divisions were engaged, but, in a few days, Col. Ward of the 2nd Florida Regiment was reported among the killed. This rendered me rather uneasy, though I still did not believe the regiment had been in the battle of Williamsburgh, but I could gain no information whatsoever.

I was returning home Tuesday evening, after having spent a very

61. The Battle of Williamsburg (May 5, 1862) and Battle of Eltham's Landing (May 7, 1862) were part of the Peninsula Campaign. The Battle of McDowell (May 8, 1862) was part of the Valley Campaign.

62. She is referring to the Battle of McDowell as the single clear Confederate victory.

fatiguing day at the ladies' kitchen, I heard that a letter was awaiting me. I hastened home, but, much to my disappointment, I found it had been written the first of May, just before the retreat commenced. But Thursday fortune smiled on me and brought me a letter written only a day or two before.

Mr. Butler was well and, much to my surprise, his regiment had been in the fight, was dreadfully cut to pieces, sixty of the men lying dead on the field. Mr. Butler, his brother, and Capt. Call escaped unharmed, and only received a covering of mud.

All of Ward's baggage was lost, so I will commence replenishing his wardrobe Monday morning. I am going to make him a fatigue shirt of my old green walking dress.

The regiment has been reorganized, Mr. Call promoted to Major. Mr. Nick has the Captaincy in his place, and, contrary to all expectation, Ward is 2nd Lieutenant in the same company. He is now acting as Regimental Adjutant and thinks he may have the position permanently.

Nothing has been heard recently of events at Corinth. Daily we have accounts of Jackson's brilliant career, but the all absorbing topic is Richmond, for upon its standing is placed the hopes of the Confederacy. If it falls, there will be one wild cry that will burst from the heart of every Southerner, and despair may come, but submission, never, for, as long as there is one strong arm in the land, it will be uplifted against the invader.

One important step seems to have been taken. The Country, the State, the Citizens have determined on no surrender but to defend the Capital to the last. And, though tardy and inefficient as have been the preparations heretofore, every effort is now made for defense, and it is believed by a few very sanguine persons that we may yet so obstruct and defend the river that the gunboats cannot ascend. If this can be effected, we do not fear them, although every effort will be made on their part to overcome us and possess themselves of the Capital.

Charlottesville. June 3, 1862

Great excitement has prevailed here during the last week: Jackson's last brilliant victory, and the retaking of Winchester, and capturing many valuable ordinances, and other stores, with four thousand prisoners. But every one is in fine spirits, and we were in daily expectation of hearing of Jackson's exploits across the Potomac.[63] We actually heard that a portion of McClellan's army had returned to defend Washington, but, alas! alas! our hopes were in vain. It is now sayed that Jackson will soon lose all that he has gained though we will trust for better things. In this great victory, there is one sad, brave, desperate act, one scarcely equalled by the charge of the "Six Hundred."[64]

Thirty-six men were riding carelessly along the road unsuspecting that the enemy was near when, suddenly, nine hundred Federal troops were disclosed to their view. A courier was instantly dispatched for orders when they received the command to advance. Not a moment was lost but on they dashed and charged the extended lines of the enemy. Many fell before them but, ere, the army came, twenty-three lay dead and wounded on the field. Helen Starke's eldest brother was among the slain. Mr. Willie Fields who is wounded in the hand is the only one of the survivors I have seen. His brother fell at his side.

Saturday afternoon I was on Main Street when a man passed and announced to his friend: "News! A telegram just arrived speaking of a general engagement near Richmond. Battle been raging all day."

We continued to hear of the fighting still going on during Sunday and Monday though we received no telegram, yet many rumors were afloat and all were under the impression that the battle was still raging and we would soon gain a complete and final victory. In the afternoon our hopes were dashed and it was sayed that only a skirmish had taken place on Saturday and we had certainly then driven the enemy back.

63. On May 23, 1862, Confederate Major General Thomas J. "Stonewall" Jackson defeated the Union forces of about a thousand at the Battle of Front Royal; nearly nine hundred Union forces surrendered. Following this victory, he headed to nearby Winchester. The First Battle of Winchester (May 25, 1862) was a Confederate victory, and Major General Nathaniel Banks and his Union forces retreated across the Potomac River into the border state of Maryland.

64. Considering Butler already quoted Tennyson in her diary, the *six hundred* likely refers to "The Charge of the Light Brigade" (1854).

I saw in the Lynchburg paper on Sunday that Hill's Division was engaged but heard no particulars. I was cheered somewhat by receiving a letter from Mr. Butler on that day though it had been written nearly a week before. He was hopeful and confident of victory and I was happy to know that the letters and package of cloathes that I sent him had reached him so soon for he must have been very uncomfortable wearing the same cloathes that he fought in at Williamsburgh for he has not been able to leave the camp long enough to procure a uniform. He must make quite a queer looking adjutant in his shabby citizen's clothes.

This morning's paper from Lynchburg gave as full an account as possible of the battle.

Saturday morning the enemy crossed the Chickahominy 30,000 strong and advanced within 6 miles of Richmond. At 2 o'clock, Hill's Division, in which Mr. Butler is stationed, made the attack, and were in the heat of the battle the rest of the day. Longstreet's and another division were engaged. They drove the enemy back across the river and a wide extended field, back through the woods, until they reached a place at which they had thrown up the breast works, where they made a stand, and many of our brave soldiers fell under the raking fire of their cannon and musketry. But we soon took their defences and they were compelled to retreat beyond their encampment and that night Our troops rested under the enemy's tents.[65]

Charlottesville. June 5, 1862

Until yesterday I heard nothing of the fate of Mr. Butler and other friends who were in the engagement of Saturday, but then we received the paper and a letter from Cousin Henry Wood which brought news more terrible than I had ever dreamed of. Captain Nick Butler and Major Call, with many other Noble brave spirits, had been sent in the

65. In the Battle of Seven Pines (May 31–June 1, 1862) both sides withstood a high number of casualties (8,000 for the Union, 5,800 for the Confederacy). Although the battle was inconclusive, the Confederates halted the Union advance.

midst of the battle from this earth. I never felt that any of them would be killed and thought the worst might be wounds, but, alas! alas! the sorrows of this war fall more heavily upon us day by day, and I feel now that soon all will be over, and that all, all that we most love will be lying cold on the battle field.

Today we received a long letter from Charlie giving a full account of the mournful occurrence.

Charlie reached the battlefield soon after the 2nd Florida Regiment had made a most desperate and successful charge. He met the servants of the Butlers' in search of the bodies of their masters who they supposed had fallen. He then found the colonel of the regiment with thirty men around him, the rest he supposed lost. But they soon rallied around him and the remnant of his men, for he came off the field with 400 men, and had lost 150, prepared to rejoin the combatants.

Charlie saw Mr. Butler who was perfectly calm and pointed out to him the bodies of his Brother and friend. He told him that they fell into a marsh waist deep and whilst struggling to extricate themselves the enemy opened a galling fire. Nick fell, leading his men on, and very soon Major Call shared the same sad fate.

Poor Dear Nick lingered for an hour perfectly conscious and died apparently peacefully. His remains were taken to the Arlington House where Mrs. Fry was so kind as to preserve some of his hair and send it to me. The next day his body was placed in Hollywood Cemetery.

This place is now suffered from a dreadful panic as it is reported by some that the enemy, three thousand strong, are at Standardsville, though this is sayed to be false by many, and that it is only a report gotten up by a frightened man who mistook a small body of our forces for the enemy. But the ladies think that the men only say this to humbug them, as they are having town meetings, etc., to consider the matter.

Charlottesville. June 9, 1862

Yesterday was a sad, solemn and sad, day and was taken up for the most part by paying the last tribute of love and respect to the dead.

Gen. Ashby, the hero Ashby, had fallen a day or two before by an unseen hand.[66] A price had long since been set on his head, and some cowardly mortal, for the love of gold, had taken his life. His remains were brought here the night before, and Sunday morning many went, I among the rest, to see the mighty dead. Cold and lifeless he lay cloathed in his military dress, his body covered with wreaths of white flowers, a sigh of sorrow ascending from every heart to think that he was lying so low.

The Company that he had at first taken into the field arrived during the day, men whom he had so bravely led on to battle with the foe, to whom he had been as gentle as a parent. Strong, hardened men wept, and sayed they loved him better than any one, even their fathers.

At 3 o'clock, the procession left the Parish House. Following the hearse was the noble black charger who moved dejectedly, with drooping head. Then the mournful horseman passed on.

The funeral services took place in the hall at the University, and were conducted by the Chaplain of the Regt. and Mr. Norton, and I heard that very fine addresses were made. The body was deposited at the university graveyard.

In the morning at 11 o'clock, Dr. Leitch's funeral took place in the Baptist church, that being the largest, and services did not take place in any other church in consequence. Every one respected and many loved the charitable Doctor. He died suddenly on Thursday night. Mr. Hoge preached a very fine though, I was told, a very long sermon, and the services were protracted still further as he was Grand Master of the Lodge here, and was buried with Masonic honours.

I saw the procession from the porch. A great number of persons were walking, but the carriages were interrupted by a number of wagons which were bringing a number of arms to the Town Hall, arms that Jackson found in Winchester.

66. The Confederate Cavalry General Turner Ashby Jr. was killed close to Harrisonburg on June 6, 1862. He was an expert horseman and was known as the "Black Knight of the Confederacy." Ashby was a Virginia native, born in Fauquier County in 1828.

We heard for several days that Jackson was retreating and that a superior force was pursuing him. Mrs. Leake passed us this morning and gave a "Hurrah, for Jackson!" and told us that he had gained a victory the day before over Fremont. We were much rejoiced, but, as more accurate accounts came, our joy departed, for we hear that some of Virginia's cavalry disgraced itself completely; most ignominiously fled before the enemy, and brought accounts of a complete route of our forces, where the authorities arrested these gallant soldiers and placed them in the guard house. The shameful conduct of the cavalry came very near causing the destruction of Jackson's army for, not being apprised of the enemy's approach, Jackson was surprised, and then he discovered his danger he found that the enemy's artillery had already been placed in position, and was compelled to storm the guns with great loss on our side. He, however, managed to drive them back, but it is feared that unless his 10,000 reinforcements reach him very soon he will be ruined.[67]

Two hundred of his wounded were brought here today, and Lydia and several of the girls are going to prepare cloathes for them tomorrow. As I am housekeeping I will have my sewing sent to me.

Merry came this afternoon and sayed that he had heard the firing of cannon all day at home. It was though Jackson was fighting again. He came for the dear little rifle which I told him he might use when he went into the service. It grieved me much to part with it, yet if it could be of any use it would have been wrong to have kept it here idle. It seems that a company are forming at Woodville to protect the arms that have been placed at Mechum's River, and to go on scouting parties, etc., if necessary.

I have been very sad and nervous since I have had time to think but will renew my labors having the house fixed for summer in the morning. This has been a holiday, Witsuntide, and the place has been

67. The Battle of Cross Keys (June 8, 1862) led to the defeat of Union major general John C. Frémont and ended in a Confederate victory. The next day, June 9, the Confederates, under the leadership of Major General Stonewall Jackson, defeated Union forces at the Battle of Port Republic.

crowded with servants from the country, all turned out in gale dress. They were much delighted with an exhibition of Yankee soldiers (some twenty of whom stopped for a while today), and they crowded around the prisoners until one of them requested the servants to "stand back and let the others get a peep."

Charlottesville. June 19, 1862

All day long have the Soldiers, Jackson's army, been passing through this place, and the town and its surroundings are still filled with them.

I was busy this morning having preserves made to send in a box to Mr. Butler, Charlie, and Bob Harper, when it was announced to me that Jackson was going past our poor little place. This very much excited and distressed me as I supposed the army was on its way to Richmond and I expected that the next soldiers we saw would be federals though now this does not seem to be apprehended, and no one knows whither the army is bound. The men themselves are ignorant. Some suppose its destination to be Alexandria, others think Madison Court House which is now occupied by the enemy.

I have heard quite often from Mr. Butler recently. He is very busy and finds it almost impossible to get leave of absence. He has only been able to go to Richmond once. Charlie is temporarily near him as he is on Gen. Garland's staff.

Farmington. July 31, 1862

How many events of interest to me have taken place since more than a month ago when I was able to make a few notes in this rather desultory diary of mine.

A few days after my last entry here I went to our old home in the country to attend to some business for Mother, wool, butter, etc., and though I was feeling badly I discharged my mission and created many reforms.

On the 25th of June, Thursday, I rode a lame Confederate horse in the heat of the day to Locust Hill. When I arrived there with a burning fever and violent headache, I felt too miserable to live, but Aunt Lucy made me go to bed and in a few days it was decided I had Typhoid fever.

Aunt Lucy nursed me with the tenderness and solicitude of a Mother, or rather as if I had been her child, for few mothers bestow such care as she did on me. Can I ever forget her kindness? For more than a week she watched and then my sisters alternately stayed with me and with the assistance of Alice nursed me very kindly and very well.

As soon as Aunt Lucy was relieved from her charge of me, Harper was laid low by the same fever, though more dangerously was he affected than I, and he is still suffering and very ill.

Charlie, who came home to recruit after the fatigue and hardships of the great battles just fought near Richmond, came to see me several times. He does not seem so much changed to me, though he is a sadder man, and, being naturally melancholy, I fear that, unless the wasted broken affections of his youth can be bound up by some teacher hand, he will become ere long a hard, cold, gloomy being.

The day I was overcome by the fever, I wrote Mr. Butler a short, ill-contrived letter for I was not well enough for the task. I told him that I was daily expecting to hear that Jackson had commenced the fight for General Lee. The next day I heard the battle had commenced the evening before and was still continued, the enemy was retreating.

After these vague reports came news that our army fought from Thursday afternoon until Tuesday night the next week. We were crowned with victory every day but many were the brave soldiers that fell.[68] I was much grieved at hearing from Mr. Butler of the death of Cousin Ebby Butler, with whom I had a short acquaintance and like him very much. His aged mother learned of her bereavement and died from the effects.

Mr. Butler was, of course, in the battle but was not engaged either the first or last day. His regiment suffered very much and so reduced are the number of officers that a captain acted as colonel, and, part of the

68. The Seven Days' Battles were a series of battles fought from June 25 to July 1, 1862. The Confederates claimed victory, and Confederate general Robert E. Lee halted Union major general George McClellan's advance to Richmond.

time, Mr. Butler had to act in that capacity. He heard from Brother Lee that he was in the battle on James Island and was highly complimented by Gen. Smith (Mr. Lee is one of his aides) for his bravery. He was almost overcome on learning the fate of our gallant Brother who, God grant, now rests in peace.

Major and Mrs. Cole have taken a house near the encampment of Longstreet, and Mr. Butler who has tried in vain to procure leave of absence begs that as soon as I am well enough to stand the journey I will accept Mrs. Cole's kind invitation immediately.

Locust Hill. September 29, 1862

I have just written the second letter today to Mr. Butler whom I heard from yesterday for the first time since the late victories in Maryland.[69] He gives a sad account of himself for he was so ill and weak after the battle that he retired to Winchester as soon as our army crossed the Potomac, and is now there in a garret without proper food as the town is crowded and a great scarcity of everything prevails. However, he intends trying to get permission to come home, but writes me not to attempt to come to see him if he should fail, as I might have to remain in the street. I should have gone notwithstanding but for the fear of passing on the road.

I was at home when I received the letter, and it would have been best perhaps to have remained there, but I felt so restless, and, as I had undertaken to teach Mollie and Harper a little too besides my own studies, I felt anxious to continue those duties, especially as I had promised to return home with Aunt Lucy. I enjoyed myself and I think Aunt Lucy and Mollie had too the few days we spent from my temporary home.

I have been reading aloud this evening the wonderful prophecy of Judge Tucker, "The Partisan Leader," a work published in 1836 which

69. The Battle of South Mountain (September 14, 1862) was a Union victory, and the Battle of Sharpsburg (Battle of Antietam; September 16–18, 1862) was inconclusive but gave the Union a strategic advantage. Antietam was the deadliest one-day battle in the war: Nearly 23,000 Union and Confederate casualties were suffered in one day.

was laughed to scorn and thrown into obscurity, but has now been brought forth, and is recognized by all who read its pages as the most marvellous foresight, even in minute matters. If it were not undoubtedly proved, few would believe but that it was by an eye-witness of this great struggle instead of a re-publication.[70]

Late. All have retired.

Locust Hill. November 27, 1862

Here once more after an absence of two months, trying to write in the early morning by firelight and make some reparation for not having done so for so long a while. I have regretted much that I have left this much abused book here as there were many things I should like to have recorded but, as usual, I have waited until the spirit of the moment has fled. I must do it no more for I am convinced that this is one great reason why this, above all other production of this genre, is dull and devoid of interest to myself, and I, am sure, would be so to anyone else could they peruse it.

Mr. Butler came from Winchester the day after I wrote my last epistle. I was at the depot when the cars passed but I did not see him. That afternoon we were summoned from Aunt Mary Lewis's by a courier as Mr. Butler and Lizzie had come. I was looking very ugly as I had a bad complexion and my hair was so thin that I confess I behaved very foolishly when they teased me about my appearance, for I had been in the country and seen so few persons that I was very sensitive.

We went home the next day and Mr. Butler's health rapidly improved and he was soon quite well and would have returned to the army but smallpox was in Staunton and in the army, so he remained until the first of November before he could be vaccinated.

Charlie returned home soon after Mr. Butler's arrival, a paroled prisoner, and Cousin William Wood came as soon as he was well enough, so we forgot the war and the trouble thereof for a short time

70. The *Partisan Leader*, originally published in 1836, describes the secession of the southern states from the Union. It was reprinted in Richmond in 1862

in our own happiness at home. We did not go away often except to take some very delightful rides as Charlie's two horses and Ward's horse were at home, besides Joe Benton's, and they were very fine ladies' horses. Mr. Butler gave me his as he had gotten one of Charlie's, and I expect to enjoy him very much as soon as he has entirely recovered his health.

Jim and Mr. Butler's servant, Bob, were the greatest heroes we had, that is, they told of many more wonderful feats they had performed than their masters did.

A week before Mr. Butler left, his cousin, Dr. Brevard, made his appearance, a fine looking, bashful, noble man he is. I became quite well acquainted with Cousin Epley. He was so gentle and affectionate that I liked him very much. The day before he left, Mr. Butler and I persuaded him to accompany us on horseback to Farmington and thence to Mr. Maury's where we dined and the day was spent most pleasantly.

The following morning Bob started off with Mr. Butler's and the doctor's horses for Staunton, the two gentlemen expecting to go to that place on the cars, and great preparations were made: three days' rations placed in their haversacks, farewells were over, and the travellers had reached the depot. In a short time after, several persons came in the house. Mr. Butler entered my room and told me that the army was at Culpepper. He had sent Cousin Epley for Bob and the horses and expected them all to be back the next day.

I went downstairs and what was my surprise at finding Carrie Morrill who had started for Maine a few days before but, finding she could not pass the lines, had returned. Then Charlie came in who had pretended he was going to Charleston but had progressed no further than Richmond, and, lastly, Father came in having returned from the Metropolis.

Dr. Brevard did not return as he is surgeon of one of Jackson's Regiments, and we learned that only Longstreet's corps was at Culpepper. Bob was detained but finally returned, and on Tuesday morning he and his mother departed, and Charlie and Jim left for Charleston the same day. Mary Woodson went to S. Carolina with Charlie to see her brother-in-law, Mr. Thomson.

Cousin William, having had the disgraceful honor of Captain in the Quartermaster Department, left for the west soon after.

I have heard from Ward several times but not since he has been at Fredericksburgh. I suppose there is but little chance of his writing from thence as both armies seem to be concentrating there and a battle is in daily expectation.

Lieutenant Lee Butler wrote quite a long letter to his brother, and, as it fell into my hands, I read it, fearing that it might not reach Ward, and then I could tell him its contents. Brother Lee had just recovered from yellow fever, and his lovely cousin, Mrs. Simpkins, had died from the effects of laudanum which an ignorant doctor had administered in too large a quantity.

Mr. Butler had begged me to write to Lee so I answered this letter and received a very kind and affectionate one in return a few days since. Lee is 1st Lieutenant of a heavy battery on James Island.

Charlie wrote me a long and interesting letter which I received and answered a week ago. He is very comfortably established in Charleston as an Adjutant General on Gen. Ripley's staff, whom he seems to like, though Capt. Earle says he is not an honourable Gentleman.

I heard from Mary Woodson too and hope we will be able to keep up the correspondence.

I waited a long while for Aunt Lucy to send or come for me, but, as she would do neither, I concluded with Nannie Maury to come anyhow. Accordingly on Tuesday morning, after many difficulties had been overcome, we found ourselves seated in the cars with Cousin G. Price and Merry as escorts, and went on, feeling quite secure and sure then that nothing could prevent our reaching the place of our destination. But, alas! alas! how little can we tell what is in store for us, and how little did we know how pleasantly we would spend the evening.

Just as we were opposite Mr. Harden's, the cars stopped, and the passengers began to look excited and to jump off the train, but I, seeing nothing either to become excited or to jump about, sat perfectly composed with Nannie when we were told that one of the cars was off the track and was broken, and perhaps the train would not start again that day.

It was now four o'clock and we began to make plans for the future, so we decided to go to Mr. Harden's and wait until Merry could go to Mr. Maury's and send a carriage for us. Before he left, he went to ask the lady whom we saw with Hunt Powell if she would accompany us, but she sayed that Capt. McPhale, her husband, was obliged to go to Staunton, and she would have to wait for the cars. We did not know Mr. Powell but knew that he was Mrs. Colston's brother, and we learned that Mrs. McPhale was his sister, a pretty young lady recently married. They soon followed us to the house where we were received by Miss Harden who, though she is an overseer's daughter, seems to have as much refinement and has as an easy manner as any lady that I know. She asked us into a very nice comfortably furnished parlor. There was quite a bond of sympathy between us as we all had short hair. A bright large fire was burning, fine apples were handed around, and we all became quite sociable, and our party was much augmented by some Gentlemen who came over. We soon found ourselves chatting familiarly about the accident that might have been serious, the sufferings of our army, the high prices of smuggled goods of which Richmond is said to be full, and any one coming in would have thought us old acquaintances, whereas not one of us had ever met before.

Mr. Powell was a friend of Lydia's and we found a good many subjects on which we could converse, mutual acquaintances, and I talked with him most of the evening.

Music was called for, the blinds closed, and lamps lighted. Miss Harden excused herself as her Mother had been sick and she could not practise. Mrs. McPhale had a sore finger, but we could not accept that as an excuse, and she played at first, and then she and her Brother sang very sweetly, and quite cured my headache.

It was dark when Reuben came with the horses, for the little carriage was in town and no suitable horses for the other carriages, but heard then that the cars would soon be able to proceed on its way rejoicing, and, as we were anxious to go on, we waited. About 8 o'clock we started off just as Miss Harden was about to have supper. We hurried on the cars quite graceful for the accident which had brought about so pleasant an evening, and we parted regretfully from our agreeable acquaintances, especially Nannie as she had found Capt. McPhale a very charming gentleman.

We found Harper awaiting us with the carriage at Woodville, and I am now comfortably established here with my school in operation. We have not heard from Merry from that day to this.

Locust Hill. November 29, 1862

We have spent this Sabbath day very quietly and pleasantly. Nannie and I read Kingsley's sermons this morning as we do every night for we are much interested in the subject and style, and are ready to proclaim Kingsley and his school as great reformers who throw aside the semblance of things and arrive at the very truth itself.

Then I read D'Aubigne's German Reformation until Major Dick Whitehead came hobbling in on his crutches with Miss Kate, and they made themselves very agreeable as they ever do.

Nannie read one of our favorite sermons to Aunt Lucy and her children, and we have now retired to our own room for the night to rest for the labors and pleasures of the morrow, for then we will resume our German, at least Nannie will assist me in that study, and our Carlyle's Frederick the Great which we are reading together, and DeQuincy, and I will commence making half a dozen Soldier's Shirts. God grant that I be able to fulfil these, and all other duties faithfully and with patience.

December 1, 1862

Weary I am for Nan and I dined at Cousin Charlie Price's in Woodville today, and I have not been sewing very hard tonight to make up for lost time.

Cousin Henry Wood who is here for a few days came over this morning and begged the use of the old gray horse so Nannie and I decked ourselves in our new hoods which fit our heads finely as they are nearly entirely divested of hair. Mine is blue, and hers, rose colour.

Nannie rode and Cousin Henry and I walked as far as Mrs. Cosby's where we called on Nelly who is quite sick, when Cousin Henry and the horse left us, and we soon after proceeded to spend the day.

Tomorrow a sale of Aunt Mary Lewis's household furniture will take place and several of the family will dine here. Nannie and I are going to the sale.

Oh! I am so sick. I must go to bed.

Locust Hill. December 8, 1862

Nannie had to go home this morning, much to my regret, for I love and admire her more than I ever have; her character morally has improved and strengthened wonderfully during the last year, and her intellect is very highly cultivated. I enjoyed the time she was with me very much.

I went to the depot with her and met Miss Kate Whitehead who has taken her final leave of us all up here. She engaged Lieut. Snyder to take a box of clothing for the society to the army, and he was so kind as to offer to take a package to Mr. Butler, consisting of his pistol, scarf, and some gloves.

I spent the morning with my pupil. Aunt Lucy was busy with her lard.

This evening I received a package from home consisting of a note from Mother and two letters from Mr. Butler, the first I have received from him since I have been here. He is still suffering from his vaccination, and I fear it will prove quite serious as he is so much exposed. He thinks that the Federal army will remain in its present position all winter, and will make desperate efforts to gain the remainder of our coast.

I asked Ward several times if he were well provided with clothing and he always assured me that he had a good supply, but now writes that he was mistaken and finds himself very deficient. I had so little time that I was afraid I could not find any socks, but Aunt Lucy was so good as to give me a pair. So I rolled up some peach leather, wrote a short letter, and Miss Burlingame called to tell us goodbye (as she intends to leave the Confederacy in a few days). She told the driver who was taking her home to call for me which he did. Merry and I jumped into the carriage and soon found ourselves in Woodville. I left the package with Lieut. Snyder and though the snow was lying on the ground and everything freezing around us we had a pleasant walk home by starlight.

Last week Aunt Mary left her old home and on Monday, no, on Wednesday, she had a sale of her household goods, stock, and grain, and the proceeds of the sale amounted to five thousand dollars, whereas two years ago five hundred would not have been realized as there was nothing handsome or of much value sold, but currency has, and is now depreciating so fearfully, and the demand for the necessities of life so great, that it is not to be wondered at.

Cousin Matilda's smart, pretty, bad daughter, and her son who is rather the opposite, except the bad, were here most of the week, and Mrs. H—— L—— with her wild eyes and crazy humor was here several days. She seems well educated, intelligent and smart—all mixed with her derangement make her very amusing and agreeable, and then, withal, she seems a sincere Christian so that with all of her eccentricities she demands respect.

Cousin Matilda seems very sad at leaving and forever giving up her old home; still she has the greatest objection to living there now, though Cousin Henry was anxious to buy the place. She intends staying at Cousin John's this winter, and, as the house is small, Cousin Margaret has given up her parlor to her for a chamber.

I succeeded in finishing my six shirts last week in spite of my numerous interruptions, but it was at the sacrifice of my literary pursuits, and by means of hard work that I accomplished the task.

I shall try regularly to establish my habits this week and as I will sleep with Aunt Lucy I know I shall have an early start tomorrow.

December 9, 1862

Merry has just been reading us an article on Lincoln's late message which surpasses in stupidity any of his or any other man's former production. Surely he is the great wonder of the age and will be preserved in Barnum's museum. It seems almost incredible that any one calling himself a man should have concocted such a collection of absurdities. The object of this document seems to be to do away with the bad effects of his emancipation proclamation which was to go into effect the first of January but I suppose the democratic elections have frightened the poor imbecile. He now declares that he has discovered a plan that will at once restore the union, satisfy his abolition friends, and, in truth, bring peace on earth, and good will toward men.

His brilliant scheme is as follows: On the immediate return of all disloyal States to allegiance to him and Mr. Seward, such States shall emancipate all slaves during the following thirty-six years, and he will indemnify them (the slave holders) by taxes raised chiefly amongst themselves. How magnanimous of him! Who can resist so generous an offer? Why none, of course not. We will be but glad to run back to him and tell him how sorry we are for being such naughty children, that we never really meant to disobey and resist him, we were only playing. Let him rest. He will find a glorious name on the pages of history with Nero and Caligula, a name preserved by his magnificent weakness and infamy.

I have not had an opportunity of studying my German today as Mollie has been sick and troublesome, but, as every one is now in bed and the house quiet, I will devote myself as long as my candle lasts.

Locust Hill. December 11, 1862

I received a nice long letter from Ward today. He seems in fine spirits and says he intends sending Bob up for his Christmas gifts. Mollie is going to give him a pig, Aunt Lucy, some eggs, and I intend to try to collect the rest of the materials to make him a nice Christmas box. I wish I could take it to him myself.

Aunt Lucy, Mollie and I are going to Farmington tomorrow, and we will have to make an early start in order to avoid the cars. I must go to bed now.

Locust Hill. December 12, 1862

We spent quite a pleasant day at Farmington. We had not been from home for so long that it was very refreshing to be out. We enjoyed the ride as the roads are good and the weather fine.

Aunt Mary and Cousin Lou were as usual as busy and as hard at work as if their daily bread depended on it. They were, notwithstanding, very kind and agreeable.

When I got back, Merry met me with the news which was rumoured yesterday: that the fighting had really commenced at Fredericksburgh.[71] Yesterday the enemy attempted to cross in three places. In two they were repulsed but effected their landing on the side of the water. Nothing more is known but it is sayed that five hundred wounded arrived in Charlottesville today. Sad, sad, will be the Christmas of some of us, even should victory be the result of the battle.

I must write to Mr. Butler tonight in the vain hope that it may reach him.

Locust Hill. December 15, 1862

The battle waged fiercely. Fredericksburgh is no more. Fighting, desperate fighting, went on Saturday, all day, and five hundred of our dear soldiers passed through the valley of the shadow of death. Many were wounded and though I stated false information when last writing, three hundred wounded were brought to Charlottesville. Gen. Cobb of Georgia was killed; Gen. Gregg badly wounded.

Every one seems to feel too much disheartened to prepare for festivities even for Christmas holidays, for it is thought that even now the bloodiest of battles is going on.

I went with the Children after hickory nuts this morning and enjoyed myself as I ever do in a ramble though the woods.

About the middle of the day Old Whitey and I went to dine at Aunt Maria's, and when I came home I found that Betty and Cousin Lucy were expected here. Betty came after a while but Cousin Lucy stayed at Cousin Charlie's.

Charlottesville. December 24, 1862

"Tis the night before Christmas," and the house which has been in a turmoil all day has at last subsided into a state of repose. The stockings

71. The Battle of Fredericksburg was fought on December 11–15, 1862. It ended in a Confederate victory led by General Robert E. Lee against Major General Ambrose Burnside. Approximately 100,000 Union forces were engaged against approximately 72,500 Confederates.

are all hung and filled, not with anything of value, but with homely Confederate presents, and many bright and happy thoughts are flitting through the brains of the children, as, besides the usual enjoyment, Lewis and Walter are to have a party.

But the rest of us have had a sad cloud thrown over our enjoyment and the usual gaieties of the season, in which we will be obliged to participate to some extent, will only make us feel sadder, for, yesterday Kate Stockton passed from earth. Whither? Oh, would that I felt more fully assured where. Poor friend, she has run her short race, and all that remains to tell us of her is her little orphaned child. Her remains will be entered tomorrow, and I shall make an effort to be present and I trust I shall be more successful than when I tried in vain to see her ere she left us.

This morning I sent Mr. Butler a Christmas box by Bob who came for it. I hope that as soon as the contents of the box is consumed that Ward will come home as he is quite lame. He had to leave the battlefield on account of the weakness in his limb.

Since Burnside's defeat at Fredericksburgh, our prospects have been daily brightening and the northern army, after committing every outrage in the poor old ruined town, has retreated to take up winter quarters in Washington. Dissention has broken out among them so strongly that if it does no permanent good, it will at least paralyze them for some time to come for Seward and Son have resigned.

I have been busy fixing Christmas greens and, with some assistance from Lydia, have decorated my room and the two parlors besides Aunt Lizzie's parlor, and, though I succeeded in making it look quite pretty, it, nevertheless tired me, and, as the night wears late, I must seek repose.

Charlottesville. December 26, 1862

The greater portion of today has been spent very delightfully for I have been making a pen and ink sketch for the frontispiece of my new journal [the frontispiece of this book features a rendering].

Yesterday, being unable to go to the funeral as I found it impossible to procure a conveyance, I went to church with Lydia and Capt. C. Carrington who bade us farewell as he was off to the wars again. Mr. Butler preached a feeling though inappropriate sermon, and, after it was over, Lydia, Ellen Maury, and I called on Mrs. Shackleford and her sister.

Then we came home and found the company just assembling at a family dinner party. Cousin Lucy was busy at the hospital and her girls excused themselves, but Carro Morrill came and the rest, and we had quite a pleasant day.

Carro and I called in the evening on Mrs. Preston and the Captain and saw John. By the time we returned home, the girls were dressing to go to an eggnog at Aunt Lizzie's, and they and Lizzie Maury looked very well, but I declined going as I felt rather sad to wish to join in any gaieties, and besides Carro refused to go. However, toward the last, I relented and told Lydia that if she would send for me late in the evening I would come. So Merry called about half past ten and I found the little assemblage had taken to amusing itself by putting each other through the painful operation of boring. Every one was every man's pincushion and very rusty pins were used. But musicians were just here introduced, dancing commenced, every one brightened, and seemed to be having a gay time.

The company consisted for the most part of funny little students. There were several grown gentleman and Major Brown who went with Gay Leake. He was the most pleasant Gentleman there, besides our party, Miss Carrington and R. Benson. I came home quite enlivened.

Carro left this morning and I am most sorry to know. Molly and Jane Price came on the cars and this evening Lewis and Walter had a most joyous party. Lewis says he kissed Mary Meade under the mistletoe and his heart feels good yet.

Lydia went to Mr. Rives's this evening to a little entertainment, and there is a party going on now at the Delevan Hospital to which most of the girls have gone, but we did not care to go (it was not for the same reason that Jack declined his meal on some occasion, as we were invited).

I must really not overlook the greatest enjoyment of Christmas, the filling and emptying stockings. We were all busy until late finishing some of our presents and then we acted the part of St. Nicholas, filling little and big stockings too for white and colored. Then grown-up stockings were placed in the front parlor and such times as we had filling them without letting the others find out.

Before light Christmas morning we heard noises and knew the children were awake. Lydia and I, decked in dressing gowns and slippers, took a light down to the back parlor, and soon came the children of all colors, shouting, firing off powdercrackers, pulling down stockings. They formed a circle around the light and a joy it was to see the happiness depicted on every countenance as they delightedly discovered some new gift.

Father and Mother had their stockings brought to their room. Father's was filled with good things, as the children would say, but really were bad things, a pair of snuffers and a bottle of cologne which I gave him.

LIST OF BOOKS READ BEGINNING AT JAN 1, 1863

Commenced		*Finis*
	Newcomes, Thackeray	Jan 14, 1863
	History of France, White	Jan 24
	Strange Story, Bulwer	Jan 28
Jan 28	*History of Girondists,* La Martine	Feb 18
Feb 18	1 vol. *Frederick the Great,* Carlyle	
	2 vol. *Frederick the Great,* Carlyle	Feb 22
		April 13
Jan.	*Sermons,* Dr. Arnold	February
Jan 27	*Sevastopol*	Jan 28
March 8	*Sermon on Resentment,* Dr. Butler	
March 14	*Hyperion,* Longfellow	March 18
March 15	2nd vol. Hist. Reformation	April 7
March 9	*Critical Essays,* Carlyle	
March 9	Jean Paul Frederick Richter	March 12
March 12	Life and Writings of Werner	March 14
March 17	Essays on Goethe	March 25
March 28	Goethe Hellina and etc., April 9	March 28
April 12	3 vo. Reformation	
April 28	*Elsie Venner,* O. W. Holmes	May 4
March	*Cain,* Byron	May 25

Charlottesville. January 12, 1863

One more unfortunate, weary of chess, for I have just been most woefully beaten by Mr. Butler who actually seems to take pleasure in beating such a poor humble creature as I, but I play on with a grim smile lighting up my countenance, with vain hope of one day learning to play the game in an artistic style.

The house is quite quiet tonight. Lydia has gone to spend the evening with some of her friends, and this morning Aunt Lucy and Mollie (who came home with Mother a week ago) left us, and took Lizzie and Aunt Susan with them. Christmas is quite over, and we have all settled down to our usual vocations which, I fear for the most part, consist in doing nothing.

In spite of the many sad events which took place during the holidays, I think we all enjoyed ourselves even during the last few days, for the girls spent a very pleasant evening with Mrs. Shackleford, and a few evenings after she and Miss Green were asked here to meet Bertha and Emma Rives who were to stay all night; and Lucy Robertson and Gay Leake, with some very agreeable and some very curious gentleman, were here, and though we did have a confederate supper it was a very pleasantly spent evening.

The great event of the New Year is the Battle of Murfreesborough where we first heard that Bragg had gained a great victory, then that he was defeated, and finally that it was a drawn battle. Certainly we can not claim a defeat when preparations are being made in Richmond to receive four thousand prisoners.[72]

I am still reading *The Newcomes* and become more attached to the book daily.

Charlottesville. January 15, 1863

Sometimes trouble after trouble, and one sad event succeeds another until we feel that the hand of death will not stop until all that we most

72. In the Battle of Stones River (December 31–January 2, 1863) the Union claimed victory despite suffering approximately 13,200 casualties (compared to 10,300 Confederate casualties).

love has been taken and our burden will be heavier than we can bear, but, blest be the name of God, this will never happen to those who trust and love Him for he will sustain them as they walk through the dark shadowed paths of life.

Our community is indeed one of mourning. After the shout of victory is stilled, the dead and wounded are brought home. Death presents itself in every form and diseases which were scarcely feared in former brighter days now present themselves as a sure messenger of death. While we tremble at the name of smallpox which is spreading surely among the citizens, we hear of the death of some sweet child of diphtheria, and this morning I must prepare to go to the funeral of Maggie Cochrane, that poor afflicted child, who died in peace, and has left a world that has been unfriendly to her after her Mother left her alone.

Charlottesville. January 28, 1863

Snow had been falling all day long and dreary and miserable indeed must be the poor sentinel as he tramps through the deep snow and comes in contact with the mud which has masked itself with so fair and pure a covering which does make beautiful this dreary old fighting winter world. The naked boughs of the trees are waving like white wands; the evergreens are so loaded that the green can scarcely be seen; and the althea cups are heaped high above their tiny rims. We have good fires, some pleasant books, and then Mr. Butler is here safe, sheltered from the storm, and we all seem to be quite enjoying life in spite of the ravages of war and disease.

I have been reading today Bulwer's last novel which succeeded in running the blockade and is now published in one of our Southern cities. "The Strange Story," as it is called, is indeed quite marvellous, a story of magic mesmerism, and treats of the occult sciences generally. It is pronounced by most of the household a failure. I have not read enough to pass judgment. I finished White's *History of France,* a book that I commenced six months ago but laid aside very frequently. I am now reading La Martine's *History of the Girondists.*

Last week, much to our surprise, Carro Morrill made her appearance early one morning, and announced her intention of starting off on the underground railroad, so she started off in a little covered wagon with other ladies. She was to travel in this way until she reached the Potomac where she would stay at the home of the old man who drove the wagon until she could cross the river and make her way home. God grant that she found kind friends and warm hearts to greet her in Maine, and that she had no trials on her way. She declared that nothing would make her take the oath to the northern government. The day she left it commenced raining and the roads have been intolerable ever since. She must have had a wearisome journey. We have scarcely realized what a loss we have sustained.

Monday, Mr. Butler and I went to Aunt Lucy's to help her eat her last turkey, and I rode my own horse. In the afternoon, we went to see Aunt Lydia now nicely settled in Uncle Lewis's old home.

We returned next morning and called at Farmington but only stayed a short time as it was already raining a little and we feared more would fall on us.

Oh, I am so glad! I beat Mr. Butler in a game of chess today.

February 5, 1863

We have a fine deep snow on the ground tonight but it has commenced raining and I fear it will all be spoiled.

Lydia is weather-bound at Farmington and Father is in Richmond so there are only Mother, Mr. Butler, and myself here, besides the boys, and we manage to keep quite comfortable.

On Sunday exciting news reached us from Charleston. The blockade had been broken by our batteries and ironclads, and we were in high hopes that the port would be opened for sixty days, as the blockade could not be resumed before that time according to the laws of nations; and brilliant uniforms, and rustling silks were already beginning to pass before our mind's eye, and striped cotton in which I am now figuring began to be looked on with disdain. But alas for all of our hopes! All of this has vanished into thin air, and I learned from today's paper that Charleston was now expecting to be beset by both sea and land by a very powerful force.

May Heaven bless her and give her strength to stand.

February 20, 1863

Thank Heaven our much loved Maggie came back to her Mother today after having been away from us for nearly two years, far away from us all, with rivers and mountains and Yankees dire between us, and we feared that her Mother might never see her more, but now she has come. I tried to get my horse and go immediately to her but Rosinante was in the country so I have been deferred seeing her until Monday. Our meeting will doubtless be as sad as it will be happy, so many changes, so many sorrows have visited us. Maggie's Grandfathers have both died since then and her Dear Uncle slain in battle, and I, I have changed my name and I fear we can never be again to each other what we have been. Oh, I am so impatient to be with her!

Mr. Butler went to Richmond this morning on business but will return tomorrow. I should have liked very much to have gone with him but he did not care for me to go. I wished to visit Mrs. Cole who is now in the Metropolis and has been there for some time, but I never had an opportunity of paying her my attention and have not yet seen her. I felt and feel anxious to know her as I have not met with any of Mr. Butler's near relatives with the exception of Dear Nick, and I feel a strange longing to know and be loved by his family though the feeling does not seem to be reciprocated.

I finished the first volume of La Martine this week and recommended *Frederick the Great* by Carlyle. I read a few pages in it some months since but had not time to finish it then. I have been illustrating my notebook this evening which is a great pet with me just now and the Newcome fever has not yet worn off so my illustrations are chiefly copies from Thackeray's illustrations.

February 22, 1863

We awoke Sunday morning to find ourselves completely blocked by the snow which had been falling all night and continued to fall most of the day, the deepest snow we have had this winter and looks as if determined to remain a long time with us and break every self-sufficient plan that we in pride and weakness have made.

I scarcely expected Mr. Butler under the circumstances yesterday, though the cars succeeded in getting here late last night, but I surely expected him today, as the cars arrived nearly as early as usual, and I am much surprised and disappointed at his non-arrival, and have been foolish enough to expect him whenever I hear the cars whistle.

I have been busily reading all day trying to finish the first volume of *Frederick the Great* which I succeeded in doing. I must plead guilty to having grown rather weary sometimes whilst Carlyle compelled me (I know much against his will) to remain in the region, Dryasdust, but the original humourous style in which even these dull subjects are treated is irresistible, and, as to the rest, where his subject is worthy of his style, I think the saying would soon be changed from "as interesting as a novel" to "as interesting as a history," if historical writers would, or rather could, adopt his easy homely powerful style. Ever and anon, amidst sarcasms and ridicule, and a rather light way of speaking, the mighty soul of the man shows itself in bursts of praise and intense admiration when he recognizes the true and earnest in a fellow being.

February 28, 1863

The last day of February and still winter is with us, with its leaden sky, chill atmosphere, and streets of liquid mud, but as disagreeable as all this is, especially the latter, it has proved this winter, and the preceding one, a strong arm of defense and most effectual barrier to the marauding hosts that hover on our borders.

I believe most persons think that the attack on Charleston will not be made, or at least deferred for some time, as disputes among the Yankee generals have frustrated their plans. Every one is hoping so ardently for peace that a great effort is being made to believe that it will come soon though I do not know what they found their hopes on except the belief that both parties are wearied out.

Mr. Butler came back on Thursday, after having had a pleasant visit, and learning that his property was safe. He was so kind as to bring me a pair of shoes for which he paid the usual price of twenty dollars. His expenses whilst in the Capital were $80, Confederate prices are startling to persons of small purses.

I have just received a note from Nannie who told me of the sad death of Johnny Maury who was drowned in the Mississippi River.

It is so dark that I cannot see to write.

Charlottesville. March 3, 1863

How like my words are to a poor picture, mere symbols or signs of the inward thought as the picture is composed of the signs of nature that would fain be imitated; though often the language I use consists of mere sounds that none of my audience can interpret and I can scarcely understand myself. Oh, would that I could express my thoughts and feelings! I believe the only feeling I have ever been able to express freely, ah, far too freely, is that of anger, and by the grace of God I hope in time to keep this under better control if I cannot extinguish it altogether. But any other feeling, any tender feeling, remains unspoken, in truth every good and generous emotion. Then the feeling becomes a chilled half defined thought, and thought remains in a troubled state there turning itself over, and striving to find utterance, when it at last escapes in cold obscure words, and I am myself startled at the strange distortion of the original feeling, and, seeing myself entirely misapprehended, I become silent when half has been said.

I must bid myself farewell now which I can do the more readily as she is by no means a fascinating personage.

And so we are to be soon pulverised by three million men so our Northern brethren tell us. The conscript bill has passed and six hundred men have already been called for. As Mr. Lincoln soon expects to be military Dictator we should be trembling in our shoes, especially as the Yankees say that Louis Napoleon is in favor of the *Union,* and, as he has taken Mexico, he will attack the southern portion of our domains and restore the Union.[73]

73. On March 3, 1863, the Union enacted the Enrollment Act. The act required the registration of all men aged twenty to forty-five, including recent immigrants, in the military.

Though we laugh at the vain boasts of our enemy, we have good cause for sadness as provisions are growing scarce—and—I must go.

Locust Hill. March 16, 1863

It snows! And I am not much delighted that such is the case for Maggie was coming here today to remain until tomorrow and, apart from selfish considerations, I regret it for I am sure she is not enjoying herself as it was only from a sense of duty that she left yesterday after our arrival in Woodville to go to Uncle Ben's. I am here for a few days to collect my cloathing which I left here as I do not ever intend to stay here again as I am not needed now for Miss Duke is coming in a few days to open a school for the benefit of the neighbourhood.

I have heard from Mr. Butler twice since he left on the 5th, and, poor fellow, he has to go back to Fredericksburgh to starve.

I had a great deal to write this morning but the ink is so thick that I cannot endure it longer.

March 19, 1863

I have just finished reading that delightful little book of Longfellow's, *Hyperion*. How it raises one from the dull commonplace current of every day life to the fairy realms of Poetry, and to talk amidst weighty thoughts with gigantic minds. It is well for the spirit of man to revel in such a flower garden for holiday now and then, but not too often or we might spend in fine thoughts time that might be employed in great actions.

One half of the world must work and groan that the other half may dream.

Before I read this Maggie did come the day after the snow and I had the pleasure of her old dear company for several days, then they heard that Miss Duke would not come until the last of this month, and they begged me to stay, but I thought I would be proud and go home, but they seemed so lonely that I consented to remain longer.

Friday I went to Uncle Tom's and had a very pleasant little stiff visit until Sunday afternoon, and, though they were all kind and polite, and Aunt Lydia was smart and agreeable, I felt that I could not longer support existence there, so I started off, and was borne on the wings of a very cold wind in a few moments to Locust Hill.

The most stirring event of the day in Woodville and its surroundings is the marriage of Jane Lewis with Dr. Walker of South Carolina, a very intelligent, agreeable young man who spent an evening at home at our house Christmas a year ago, when I was much pleased with him, and have never seen him since. Jane met him in Petersburgh during the past winter where he was practicing as a surgeon in a hospital. He is still stationed there, and Jane will not have to suffer the sad parting nor will she feel the happiness of reunion that most of us war time brides have been called to bear.

The wedding took place in the morning, the bride arrayed in handsome traveling costume, a dark bride surrounded by weeping friends, a few of whom were present; a dark day with clouds threatening to act as indiscreetly as the friends, most of whom returned home, sad, cold, and hungry, for no refreshments were present which, alone, can form the consummation of happiness to most of the juvenile part of the company.

Yesterday this great little event occurred and the party is now en route for Carolina on a visit. All is quiet up here tonight, so still and calm, and snow has fallen and covered all traces of passing footsteps. The only communication we hold with the outer world is through the medium of the daily paper which gives us today an account of the skirmish, or rather a battle, that occurred during the past few days on the Rappahannock. The enemy were repulsed, leaving their dead and wounded this side of the river, though they had a superior force to Gen. Fitzhugh Lee's cavalry who beat them, and they had artillery.[74]

Monday afternoon I walked to Woodville to see the Browns on business and to talk with Cousin Charlie Price about my horse. He promised to fatten him for me, and, if I wished, to sell him, and I sup-

74. The Battle of Kelly's Ford (March 17, 1863) was inconclusive: The Union cavalry first attacked and then was repelled by the Confederate cavalry led by Brigadier General Fitzhugh Lee.

pose I must have this done though it grieves my heart to think it. I have had such delightful rides on him real and imaginary.

After the horse discussion he handed me a letter which I recognized instantly. I read it on the porch in the cold. It was a very dear letter to me though it told of the hardships and sufferings that Ward was undergoing, I know so patiently and calmly.

I came home lighter hearted though sad, but Cousin Charlie and Alice came home with us and discussed the wedding and grew quite cheerful and merry, especially as they both discussed the dilapidated conditions of their wardrobes, and how unprepared they were for such an event.

I offered Cousin Alice my walking dress, the only one I brought with me, which is decided in the sere and yellow leaf, which she accepted quite gladly, so I had the pleasure of sending my dress if I could not go myself. Cousin Charlie bewailed his sad fate at not having a black coat. I told him Mr. Butler had a very nice one that he wore every day when at home which he was welcome to wear, or his best one was at his service if he would send for it. He came up quite triumphant after the wedding and reported that he made a finer appearance in the every day coat and his pantaloons on which he wasted a bottle of ink that any one present.

I am writing so badly by this poor light that I will wait until I am less disturbed and can see better.

Locust Hill. March 25, 1863

We have been favored with one partially bright day which we took advantage of, and, in company with Merry, I rode out this afternoon. I felt weak and badly for I have suffered bad health for some time, but the fresh air soon invigorated me, and we went up to the very summit of Turner's mountain where we would see through the naked branches of the trees entirely around us. The mountains seemed to form a complete circle and were at every point the boundary line. They rose dark and grand before us, then came woodland tracts, then hills swirling and rolling up towards the mountains as though they would like to join the frowning band, but all was cheerless and barren: a few fields of pale yellow dead grass here and there; the rest, red or sad colored plowed ground, not a green hill to be seen. Grand and desolate was it all.

We came home through Woodville which was crowded with men as the cars had just passed by, and whilst there Dr. Woods and his cousin, Warwick, had a quarrel, or rather, had a mutual insulting contest.

I heard from Maggie today and she is going home with me next week.

Locust Hill. March 28, 1863

Many thoughts have suggested themselves to my mind but I felt too sad and had too little energy to record them.

On yesterday we went to church to observe the great national fast day, a day of solemn prayer and fasting appointed by President Davis, a day on which this much afflicted nation should send up petitions for peace and freedom.[75]

I was so fortunate as to get a letter yesterday and today from Ward which served to cheer me to some extent.

Weary, weak, and miserable, I go to rest, and may the morrow bring rest unto my soul.

Charlottesville. April 13, 1863

I have just finished reading the second volume of *Frederick the Great,* and I supposed that then I should have finished with the work, but I find that there are several other volumes, and that Carlyle has not yet completed it. I cannot admire Carlyle as a historian, certainly he excels in other branches of literature far more than in this, though he writes so clearly, or rather seems to have a clear insight into everything himself. How sarcastically and yet kindly too sometimes he deals with the great ones of the earth.

I came home and Maggie with me on Saturday a week ago. We found Nannie and Betty here and spent some very pleasant days with them but they have all gone now.

The great event of the day is the attack on Charleston. We heard of the impending conflict the first of the week, and on Thursday came the

75. Jefferson Davis declared nine official days of fasting throughout the war; see nn. 19, 41, and 52 in "Diary."

news that an attack had been made by gun boats which we repulsed, sinking one of the enemy's finest vessels. After which they retired, and we have heard of no fresh movements on their part, though we are in daily expectation of hearing of the renewal of the attack.[76]

May 2, 1863

After nearly two weeks sickness, I am again able to write a few lines though I am not yet well enough to leave my bed.

These two first days in May have been very lovely, that is, if we had not internal as well as external lives to lead, for all were much agitated by recent events: a great battle in expectation at Fredericksburgh for several days, but the enemy have taken a part of the railroad so that we can hear nothing. An advance has been made in the direction of Gordonsville but we have nine thousand men there, and I trust that the fears of some are groundless who dread an attack here.

May 3, 1863

The church bells have ceased to send forth their peaceful cheerful peals, but, hark! There is another bell, harsh, quick is its ring. That is no church bell. No! It is the tocsin, and old men and boys are called to arms! The enemy is near, at Gordonsville they say that fighting is going on, and it is thought that hostile forces will march up as far as Cobham in order to attack Gordonsville advantageously. But I cannot learn much as I only overhear what is said in the passages and what Alice tells me, and then I am lying on my sofa today, near the window, and can see the people passing by.

First came the young girls and their mothers, and very old men, quietly walking to church in their new spring cloathes, or rather, in their renovated old ones; and then the hurrying crowd, ladies and children on the sidewalks on their way to the depot so as to be off to Lynchburgh as soon as possible; the middle of the street thronged with refugees,

76. In the First Battle of Charleston Harbor (April 7, 1863) the USS *Keokuk* was sunk, and the Confederates gained the victory.

usually in this order: the white family in carriages, then one or two wagons full of coloured women and children, a wagon of forage for the horses and cattle that follow in the rear; baggage, wagons, men on horseback riding furiously about; and agitators in the form of several worthy women of the town rushing round like mad.

I hear now that it is thought seriously that the Yankees will make an attack on the road between here and Lynchburgh, but I expect I have here given a most wonderfully contradictory account as nearly every one that comes tells a different story.

It is afternoon now and Harper tells me that the Hampton Brigade is expected here this evening. They are no great distance off and I hope they will come.

Snowden came in about dinner time and informed me that he intended to join the town troops with or without parents' permission, so I gave him my rifle. He made some cartridges and started off, but Charley Harmon came for the rifle and Snowden reluctantly gave it up.

Two companies were sent out early in the day, one to Monticello, the other to the railroad bridge; a third party went this afternoon to the common road bridge. I am rejoiced that one Southern town, and that my own, should make some resistance. I am proud of the plan though I may have to blush for it in a few hours. I pray not.

If I ever wish to read this, I must excuse it for I have often been interrupted by persons, and have had to stop from my own weakness.

May 7, 1863

Mr. Earle has just been here with Betty, but Mother would not let me go down to see him, so I consoled myself with a cry for I am becoming very babyish. But they are coming tomorrow and I hope to see them.

Two of Mr. Butler's cousins are in town but I am afraid I shall not see them.

We have just recovered this morning from a second panic for we had a worse one yesterday than ever, and I would not be surprised if we had another before night. I hope not, for it is very fatiguing, and the poor old ladies, I am sure, are tired of putting away in a safe place their plate consisting of spoons.

We heard yesterday of a great victory gained at Fredericksburgh, and I am very anxious to hear from Mr. Butler. I received a letter written by him a week or more ago, and he was then very confident of a victory. Jackson won a victory a few days since but we heard yesterday that he had been wounded badly, and his arm had been amputated at the shoulder which is regarded as the greatest misfortune, next to his death, that could have befallen the cause.[77]

July 3, 1863

Just two years since tonight I was a bride. A few kind friends stood around me; a great comet, herald of bloodshed and strife, glared half athwart the sky; and yet, though many had already rushed to arms, we were too happy to take warning. Since that night, four of the little company have been taken to their final resting place, two fell in defense of their country's cause, and rivers of blood have been poured forth, and I, I am left alone without hope save in the grave which God be thanked must come some day.

77. The Second Battle of Fredericksburg (May 3, 1863) was a Union victory; the Battle of Chancellorsville (April 30–May 6, 1863) was a Confederate victory. Major General Stonewall Jackson lost his left arm at Chancellorsville and died on May 10 of complications from pneumonia.

Index